SPIRIT
— IN THE —
STONE

A HANDBOOK OF SOUTHWEST INDIAN ANIMAL CARVINGS AND BELIEFS

Dearest Susan,

I know how much you loved Cathy & her wonderful spirit. I thought of you today when I was shopping with Sara & thought a fetish might be appropriate. Let her spirit constantly surround you, comfort you & give you lifelong positive direction.

All My Love
always,

John

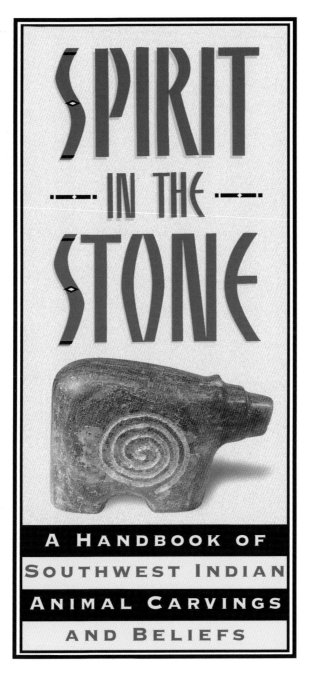

SPIRIT IN THE STONE

STONE

A HANDBOOK OF SOUTHWEST INDIAN ANIMAL CARVINGS AND BELIEFS

MARK BAHTI

TREASURE CHEST BOOKS

Treasure Chest Books
P. O. Box 5250
Tucson, AZ 85703-0250
(520) 623-9558

ISBN 1-887896-09-0

A portion of the proceeds of this book is donated to the General Fund of the Tucson Indian
Center, a predominantly Indian-directed and -operated organization serving the urban Indian
community of Pima County, Arizona.

This book is set in Stone Print Roman.
Edited by Linnea Gentry
Designed by Sullivan Scully Design Group
Printed in China

*Zuni crane made of mother-of-pearl
by Fabian Tsethlikai*

TABLE OF CONTENTS

PREFACE

There has always been a borrowing back and forth among most Indian cultures. And what was borrowed was not only adopted, but adapted in the process. The Indian cultures involved in these exchanges, for all their differences, shared some important fundamental similarities. Chief among them was a world view in which all things possessed a spirit. Even inanimate objects, such as the earth itself (Mother Earth), were conceptualized as living beings. In this world, humankind was no more important or deserving of respect than any other element. And to survive in that world, humans had to learn to understand and harmonize with it.

In recent years, a growing number of Euro-Americans have borrowed elements from various Indian cultures and tried to incorporate them into their own cultural systems. Though no harm has been intended, many in the Indian community feel exploited and are speaking out against such practices. Prominent among their objections are the appearance of seminars professing to teach — for a fee — traditional shamanism, the advent of non-Indians claiming to be Indians and also claiming Indian spirit guides (who curiously communicate in English, not in their native language), and a variety of attempts to commercialize traditional Indian beliefs, rites, and religious objects. Both Indians and non-Indians have joined in the heated debate on this cross-cultural issue.

The debate often reveals the sad fact that many people are unaware of the foundations behind the belief systems of the many Native American groups. Among most tribes, religious knowledge is not a commodity to be sold or bartered. A prayer or rite is not just something to be learned; it must be acquired by legitimate means from someone with the right to teach it. For most Indian religions, a rite performed outside its traditional and original cultural context is a rite without meaning or purpose.

Every family, every culture has its traditions, its values, its strengths which provide a source of spirituality. When investigating the traditions and strengths of other cultures, we can enrich ourselves and our own culture by learning about and learning from others without borrowing out of context and thereby trivializing those cultures we intend to learn from. It is one thing to adopt a concept and quite another to adopt a specific rite that is an integral and inseparable part of another religious lifeway.

This book explains some of the general purposes and uses of fetishes, charms, and amulets made by various Southwest Indian tribes. There are a considerable number of animal carvings being made today, however, that are not nor have ever been used in any religious context. They are not traditional in any sense of the word; but there are traditional stories and beliefs surrounding many of the animals themselves, and those are included here.

*Editor's Note: All words in a Native American language are set in **boldface** type the first time they appear and in normal roman type thereafter.*

ACKNOWLEDGMENTS

A number of people have been helpful in ways large and small, but all important. Among those I need to thank for sharing their knowledge and insight is my brother, Kurt Bahti, who helped me avoid repeating a number of common misconceptions about birds and animals of North America. In addition, Dr. Wade Sherbrooke (an expert on horned lizards) of the Southwestern Research Station of the American Museum of Natural History in Portal, Arizona, and Dr. Donna J. Howell (an expert on bats) willingly shared with me their storehouses of ethnographic information in their areas of expertise. Dr. Edgar J. McCullough of the University of Arizona was enormously helpful in unraveling the identity, correct chemical structure, and classifications of the minerals used by carvers. Among others who provided me with information and direction are Alan Ferg of the Arizona State Museum, Dr. Jane M. Young of the University of New Mexico, and Dr. Kelly Hays-Gilpin of Northern Arizona University.

Vocabulary from the languages of the various tribes discussed here has been included to emphasize that the customs and beliefs cited are part of a much larger whole, a way of life that is embodied in the language itself. Extremely helpful in this aspect were: Dr. Emory Sekaquaptewa of the University of Arizona, who provided his expertise in the Hopi language as spoken on Third Mesa, and Dr. Ed Ladd of the Museum of New Mexico, who shared his knowledge of the Zuni language and provided keen insight into Zuni concepts commonly (if not always accurately) repeated in some of the more popular texts. Conversations with each helped me keep in mind that some information about religious beliefs and practices is not appropriate for the public domain. Alex Beeshligaii and Geneva John helped me with the Navajo language, reminding me of its richness and complexity. For Tohono O'odham vocabulary, Andrea Ramon, her mother Frances A. Garcia, and her grandmother Hilda K. Garcia were most helpful. For Yaqui vocabulary, Bill Quiroga kindly lent his help.

Dr. Karl Pribam, through his wife Katherine Neville, provided me with direction in seeking to understand how fetishes may assist the human mind in achieving the requested goals. Helpful in identifying carvers, dating work, and acquiring examples of their work were Ken Baxstrom, Corilee Sanders, Michael Dunham, Scott Ryerson, Mr. And Mrs. Boyd Walker, Georgianna Kennedy, Milford Nahohai, Kent and Laurie McManis, Marian Rodee, Morton Sachs, Joe and Jan Douthitt, Ken Tafoya, Kim Messier, O. T. Branson, Ethel Branson, as well as many of the carvers themselves, including Andres Quam, Mike Romero, Ron Upshaw, Dale Lucio, Frank Mapatie, Herbert Him, Marvin Pinto, and Roseanne Ghahate.

Linnea Gentry's work as editor, improving and clarifying the text, was invaluable. Providing useful suggestions as the text evolved were the late Polly Bircher, Traci Morris, Deborah Zeller, and my wife, Dolores Rivas Bahti. Thanks are due to photographer David Burckhalter, who approached his work with conscientious good nature.

A special acknowledgement is due my younger son, Santiago, who accompanied me on all my trips, making them special for me and for all whom we visited.

PART I

THE ROLE OF THE FETISH

Naturally shaped stone resembling an animal

THE ROLE OF THE FETISH

Call them fetishes, charms, amulets, talismans, or simply good luck pieces, virtually every culture has them. In contemporary Euro-American cultures, the best-known ones include such diverse items as a horseshoe for general good luck, a rabbit's foot for a more portable source of good luck, and a St. Christopher medal for safety while traveling.

> *What animal's sharp sight have I*
> *for my sharp sight?*
> *The Gull's sharp sight have I*
> *for my sharp sight!*
>
> —AMMASSAHK ESKIMO SONG
> (From Rasmussen,
> THE NETSALIK ESKIMO*)

In Western Europe in the thirteenth and fourteenth centuries, people used fetishes or amulets with many names and in many forms. In Italy they used triangular pieces of malachite to ward off the Evil Eye, a task also assigned to the rooster. An amethyst with a bear image put demons to flight (as did the bat) and was a charm against drunkenness. A frog image in amethyst could reconcile enemies, a garnet with a lion image could protect travelers, and red jasper with the image of a stag helped to heal. A different creature presided over each day of the week, beginning with the lion on Sunday and proceeding with the ermine, lynx, fox, bull, goat, and hog, each in turn representing an ancient deity associated with that day. (See Chart A in the appendix.)

Non-Indian bear

*See References in appendix for full citation.

As with other cultures, our beliefs have also changed, some evolving over centuries and others over relatively short periods of time. Many people at the turn of the century regarded diamonds as bad luck, but a skillful advertising campaign succeeded in dispelling that myth and creating a new one—that diamonds are the appropriate symbols for engagement and wedding ceremonies.

Despite this fascinating and diverse lore, many have either forgotten most of it or no longer have any faith in it, apparently finding the charms, fetishes, and amulets of other cultures more compelling and effective for their needs. Additionally, some may be interested in them for what they tell us of the cultures that create and use them. Others may be drawn to their artistic qualities, their intrinsic value, or even simply as a memento of a visit to another region, another culture—a reminder of something experienced, something learned during that time. Regardless of the reason, learning about the background of such material objects can teach us about the people of other cultures. And often we find that we learn more about ourselves in the bargain. The following pages provide just such a glimpse into the world view of another people.

OBJECTS OF POWER

Fetish is a poor English equivalent for a concept which has a different name and even a somewhat different meaning in each language of the Native American tribes that use such objects. Even in a single culture, such as the Zuni, there are many different categories of fetishes. **Wema:we** (WEH-mah'-weh) means "prey animals" in Zuni, but in recent years it has been

> *I know what it means in Zuni, but. . .*
>
> — DR. EDMUND LADD,
> ZUNI SCHOLAR

given a secondary meaning referring to the fetishes or animal carvings sold in shops on and off the Zuni Reservation.

The other term sometimes used in this context in Zuni is **weme** (WEH-meh), which is a hunting charm that is found, not made.

The Iroquois equivalent of fetish is **ochi-na-kenda** (oh-chee-NA-ken-dah), which refers to any object possessing consciousness, will, immortal life, and magic power. Such objects can accomplish the usual and unusual by mysterious means. At the risk of oversimplifying, we can think of a fetish as an object containing a spirit that provides supernatural assistance if treated with proper respect. This definition also helps determine the difference between a fetish and a carving: if you believe it is a fetish, it is. If you don't, it isn't, since a fetish spirit will not help an unbelieving owner.

Zuni religious tradition records a legend about how certain fetishes came to be. The basic version begins when the world was wet and muddy. This unstable

Zuni figurine of a priest, made of antler by Anderson Weahkee

earth had to be dried and hardened. The task was done by the twin sons of the Sun Father. They shot lightning to the four corners of the world. In the process, the animals of prey that threatened the existence of humans were petrified into stone. In a translation by the ethnologist Frank Cushing, the Zuni Twins told these stone animals, "That ye may not be evil unto men, but that ye may be a great good unto them, have we changed you into rock everlasting. By the magic breath of prey, by the heart that shall endure forever within you, shall ye be made to serve instead of to devour mankind."

Simple possession of a fetish is insufficient to provide the owner with aid or protection. At the very least there are prayers to intone or an offering to be made. The Navajo **jish** (pronounced as written, with an English j) is an assemblage of sacred objects that can cure or protect. They generally contain a fetish and include herbs, rattles, whistles, cords, arrowheads, reeds, and paint or pollen, among other items. The fetish is effective only within the proper ritual context, with the correct prayers spoken in the native language. It is also important to understand that while a Zuni may carve a llama which is purchased by someone who treats or regards it as a fetish, that does not make the object a Zuni llama fetish. It is simply a Zuni llama carving that has become someone else's fetish.

Hunter, computer programmer, farmer, or investor—what do fetishes do for these owners? Three-dimensional mental images organize information in the mind more efficiently than words alone and keep the brain more alert to changes and new information. These images are highly complex in their bits and pieces, but simple in their unity. For example, if you were to try and memorize

Navajo bear

a list of every object in your home and the distances between pieces of furniture, paintings, doors, etc., you would likely be overwhelmed by the task. But if you were to close your eyes and take an imaginary walk through your home, you would "see" everything there in the three-dimensional model because your brain has organized them into a single and easy-to-remember mental image.

Fetishes can serve similar mental purposes. For an early hunter, a mountain lion fetish may have helped him focus on hunting, organizing all the crucial details into the most efficient way to approach the goal. Such an object aids concentration. Whether one believes in the fetish's ability to help or not, there is still the benefit of focusing the remarkable and undeniable power of one's mind more effectively on a specific task or goal.

Fetishes may be given offerings to solicit or encourage their help, but they are not prayed to. Prayer in most Indian cultures is directed towards a deity or deities. When offered correctly, down to the tiniest detail and with a clear heart, prayer *compels* the gods to answer. It is not a supplication. Interestingly, many of the recorded ritual prayers of the Native American peoples are meant to bring blessings to all, not just the person uttering the prayer.

DIRECTIONS & COLORS

North American Indian tribes have long used the compass directions to organize both the physical and the spiritual world. Depending upon the tribe, the
number of recognized directions can include the four cardinal directions or
even five, six, and seven with the addition of the zenith, the nadir, and the
middle. (The Zuni often refer to the site of their village as **Itiwanna**, the
Middle Place.) The directions sometimes have phenomena associated with
them, such as colors, seasons, animals, and plants. Although each direction
usually has a unique attribute, an element may occasionally be repeated for
the opposite direction.

Most American Indian tribes name the cardinal directions in a "sunwise"
manner, beginning with the east—the most sacred direction—then south,
then west, then north. (The practice of going in a sunwise direction was
followed also by the earliest European clockmakers who modeled their clocks
on the motion of sundials, which were dictated by the path of the sun itself, a
motion we have come to call "clockwise.") In religious rituals, however, the
naming of the directions will generally begin in the north, going counter-clock-
wise to end in the sacred east. Not all tribes
recognize four cardinal points. In some Tiwa
pueblos, there are five cardinal directions,
proceeding north, west, south, east,
and between east and north
(called **pima**).

*Isleta bear made of
alabaster by Andy Abeita*

Animals are often assigned
to particular directions. They
can also be grouped according to season or
time of day. Night animals include the owl

Isleta corn maiden made of alabaster by Andy Abeita

and bat. Summer animals include the frog, turtle, badger, joining the Sun, tobacco, and First Grass. Winter animals are bear, coyote, deer, turkey, crane, and grouse. Bear, crane, and grouse not only control or bring winter; they can also help ward off winter illness or any other dangers that the winter season might bring. Among the Tewa pueblos, corn maidens, trees, water serpents, and water sources can also be associated with each direction.

Colors can indicate other features. They can chart the movement of the sun, from white dawn to yellow to red sunset. Among the Navajo, green turquoise is regarded as female and blue as male, although this does not restrict the color of turquoise that a Navajo male or female may wear. The Hopi distinguish between the male and female **Shalako katsinas** (SHAH-lah-ko ka-TSEE-nahs), or spirit beings, by painting the face of the male pink and that of the female white. At Acoma, a male antelope may be depicted in pink and the female in yellow. In some contexts among the Apache, yellow is associated with a state of holiness because it is the color of sacred corn pollen.

The development of directional concepts and their importance varies from tribe to tribe. Chart B in the appendix shows the directions and their colors, along with other attributes assigned by various tribes. More than one color arrangement may be recognized within a given tribe. The type of ceremony and time of year may also require a change in color or color sequence.

THE ZUNI

The Zuni, who call themselves **Ashiwi** (ah-SHEE-wee, which they write A:shiwi), are a Pueblo Indian people of about 9,000 living in and around the pueblo of Zuni in western New Mexico. They speak a language unrelated to any other Indian group in the Southwest. Their religion is complex and intricate and includes six sects: the Sun, the Rainmakers (which has twelve priesthoods), the **Kokko** (spirit beings similar to the katsinas* of the Hopi), Priests of the Kokko, War Gods, and Animal Beings (a sect which has twelve related curing societies), each with its own religious calendar priests and rites. Zuni philosophy holds that human existence lies within the larger context of the spirit world, which is controlled by the spirit beings and another group of beings who are "the keepers of our life's roads." Not surprisingly, their use of fetishes is equally extensive and complex. The

Zuni otter made of pipestone by Justin Red Elk

most commonly used fetish among the Zuni is the **mille** (MEE-lee), a personal fetish given to an individual at the time of initiation into a religious society, which is then kept for life. It is made from a perfect ear of corn with feathers attached. On the other end of the spectrum are those fetishes belonging to a single practitioner within one of the six religious societies and those belonging to the entire tribe. Some are kept only for the life of the owner. Other fetishes have remained in tribal ownership since the beginning of Zuni history.

Spirit beings who appear in masked ceremonies in many pueblos. Katsina is their Hopi name.

The latter include the smallest but perhaps most sacred category: those said to have been gifts from the gods themselves.

Among these, the **ettone** (EH-tone-eh) is associated with the beings known as the Rainmakers and is perhaps the single most important fetish among the Zuni. It is composed of a reed bundle bound with cotton string. Other fetishes (which generally include a bowl and often other items) are owned by a religious practitioner or a society. Each fetish has its specific purpose, ranging from protection against witchcraft to controlling the weather, luck in gambling, use in war ceremonials, and curing illnesses.

Unusually shaped stones and natural concretions are among the most sought after, valued for their natural similarity to animals, supernatural beings, or internal organs. Before they can be used as fetishes, they must go through the appropriate ritual with a Zuni priest. They have sacred plumes attached, along with necklaces of shell and stone beads. Other fetishes are carved (and sometimes painted) animals of stone or shell. The line carved or inlaid on some Zuni fetishes is called by various names, including "spirit line," "breath line," and "heartline." There is no word for it in the Zuni tongue.

Zuni hummingbird made of green snail shell by Carlos Tsattie

Zuni fetishes are sometimes stored in jars, resting on a bed of cotton or down, and are periodically "fed" corn meal, ground turquoise or shell, or corn pollen. The top of the bowl is usually covered with buckskin. The feeding takes place through a small hole (one to four inches in diameter) in the side of the jar, which permits passage of a feather (usually from an eagle) carrying the food on its tip. The jar used to hold the

> *My Fathers*
> *I ask you for life.*
> *May my children's roads all be fulfilled;*
> *May they grow old*
> *May their roads reach all the way to*
> *Dawn Lake*
> *May their roads be fulfilled.*
>
> ZUNI PRAYER
> (From Bunzel,
> ZUNI CEREMONIALISM)

ettowe (plural of ettone) fetishes has no opening nor any outward indication of its contents. Individually owned fetishes may be kept in a pouch, on a shelf, in a drawer, worn around the neck, tied to a belt, or carried in the hand or mouth, depending upon circumstances.

Fetishes may be washed or repainted as needed or as required by the religious calendar. Some may be renewed by offerings that are poured over or otherwise applied to the fetish object. The winter solstice is the time of fetish renewal, along with other customary Zuni religious observances.

In the past, there were probably no more than a dozen individuals at Zuni who carved fetishes either for Zuni consumption or for trade with other tribes. The advent of Anglo collectors presented a new market in the 1920s, a market that grew slowly until the 1960s when so-called "fetish" necklaces gained popularity. (From the standpoint of Zuni religion, fetishes by definition cannot be jewelry.) By the late 1980s the number of carvers had risen dramatically. At the time of this writing, there are approximately three hundred Zunis carving fetishes part- or full-time.

THE RIO GRANDE PUEBLOS

The Rio Grande pueblos,* all located in the state of New Mexico and most of them in the Rio Grande river valley, consist of four linguistic groups:

1. the **Tiwa**-speaking pueblos of Isleta, Taos, Picuris, and Sandia;
2. the **Keresan**-speaking pueblos of Zia, Santo Domingo, Santa Ana, San Felipe, Cochiti and, to the west, Laguna and Acoma;
3. the **Tewa**-speaking pueblos of Santa Clara, San Juan, San Ildefonso, Tesuque, Nambé, and Pojoaque;
4. the only remaining pueblo where **Towa** is spoken, Jemez.

Among the Keresan Indians, fetishes are called **yaya** by some and **koh-pirshtai-ah** (koh-PIRSH-tay-ah) by others. Koh-pirshtai-ah means "spirit beings," a category that includes katsinas and deities. Fetishes used among the Keresan range from those owned by individuals to those unique objects held by a **cacique** (kaa-SEEK-kay, a priest), such as the large Cochiti **shtehyah-monyi** stone carving which is dressed with shell and turquoise beads and surrounded by smaller animal fetishes during religious observances. Participants in the ceremonies touch it or draw a breath from close

Santo Domingo bear made of turquoise by Walter Garcia

*A word to the reader about the uses and meanings of the Spanish word "pueblo," meaning village or town: When written with a lower case p, the word pueblo refers to the village and its adjoining land that is the home place of the group under discussion. When written with a capital P, the word Pueblo refers to the Indian group as a tribe, a people, whose proper name is the Pueblo Indians.

proximity to acquire power, a power best described as "life force." Caciques are also in charge of fetish stones that are called mountain effigies.

Among most Pueblo peoples, each person has a corn fetish, kept for life. It is made of a perfect ear of corn and called **Iarrikko** (ee-AR-ree-ko). At Cochiti, an ear of blue corn is used. Use of individual fetishes varies.

Isleta corn maiden made of serpentine by Andy Abeita

May you be happy without tears
May you be calm without sorrow
May you be content without loneliness
May you continue to be loved and liked
May you have your goal in life:
May you gain life of abundance.
May it be so!

TEWA PRAYER
(From Laski, "SEEKING LIFE")

Because the puma is reputed to have the ability to actually will game to come to it, hunters sometimes carry a puma fetish, usually in a small pouch along with corn meal and crushed shell and turquoise. At Taos, the most highly prized puma fetish is made from a calcerous deposit (called bezoar) sometimes found in the stomach of a deer. Cochiti still maintains a puma shrine with two large stone pumas. The pueblos of Zia, Acoma, and Laguna also found the puma useful for its curative abilities, especially for injuries resulting from hunting accidents. At Santo Domingo, the puma was the hunter and the bear was associated with warfare. For those from Laguna hunting the puma, the proper fetish was the snake, the only creature considered to be faster.

At the Tiwa pueblo of Isleta five animals were associated with healing: puma, bear, eagle, badger, and rattlesnake. Crystals were used to invoke or represent the moon. Both at Isleta and at many other pueblos along the Rio Grande, caciques used crystals to find lost objects or to locate game. Traditionally, caciques often made a fetish if the need arose. They also kept the highly prized concretion fetishes of unusual and distinctive forms. The Tewa caciques still use a

Nambé - Pojoaqué bison made of alabaster by Lawrence Perez

fetish called a **ciwi-kah** (see-WEE-kah) in a variety of blessings and ceremonies. It is made from a perfect ear of white corn with particular feathers attached. A Corn Mother is another important fetish that belongs to the pueblo as a whole, as vital to their spiritual well being as corn was to their physical well being. It is wrapped with shell and stone beads with feathers attached.

Stone fetishes resembling an ear of corn and representing or symbolizing the power of the Corn Mother were once widely held among the pueblos. In some instances, the eyes and mouths would be carved and inlaid with turquoise or shell. In other cases, the tapered cylindrical stone would simply be dressed in shell and stone beads and wrapped with the appropriate feathers. It is most probable that the stone objects found in ancient pueblo sites and once listed as "phallic objects" are, ironically, Corn Mothers.

Arrowheads, widely used as a general protection against evil, including witchcraft, are also used by caciques for personal protection while performing certain ceremonies. In the past, a runner from Isleta sometimes carried a white arrowhead in his mouth for protection while running.

Taos cow made of clay

Cochiti raven/crow made of basalt stone by Salvador Romero

Another category is those fetishes associated with livestock protection. Livestock fetishes are often made of clay and used as offerings in conjunction with certain annual rites. At Taos, there is a winter solstice ceremony in which clay animals are made for the portion of the ceremony intended to maintain or increase the herds of domestic and game animals. Most pueblos hold similar observances, often at Christmas or the winter solstice, in which the figurines of livestock are buried in or next to the animals' corrals. The use of stone and shell livestock fetishes is not widespread, but appears to be on the upswing in the last few years.

At a number of Rio Grande pueblos, use of fetishes has dwindled and is now largely limited to the personal fetishes made from corn and those used by the remaining medicine men. Hunting fetishes, usually a mountain lion, are still occasionally used. The sacred site at Cochiti containing the carved stone mountain lions, a victim of declining usage and occasional vandalism for many years, has recently been renewed and is now regularly visited and protected by hunters from Cochiti and other nearby pueblos. The rise in general interest in fetishes has, to some extent, revived personal use among members of some Pueblo groups. The most widely owned animal fetish is probably the bear, carried for personal protection or strength. Most of these fetishes are made by Zuni or Navajo carvers, as only a few fetish carvers are active among the Rio Grande pueblos at this time. It is not known if any of the carvers are caciques, in keeping with the earlier traditions.

THE HOPI

Among the Hopi, fetishes have been associated traditionally with healing, livestock fertility, and the protection of crops, villages, or individuals. Their religious societies use certain unusual stone concretions and formations representing such important divine beings as Spiderwoman and the Twin War Gods in connection with ceremonies. These objects do not, however, meet the definition of a fetish, charm, or amulet. Other communally owned fetish objects include the **tiponi** (tee-POH-nee), whose appearance varies depending upon the clan or society that owns it. At its center might be an ear of corn or cornmeal and seeds wrapped in a cornhusk and the entirety enclosed in buckskin with feathers attached.

An old-style Hopi broom, looking much like a whisk, was sometimes placed on or next to a baby's cradle to keep away possible sources of illness, such as witchcraft. Stones that resemble mountains (called **tukwi**, TOOK-wee) were sometimes used on religious altars and in corn bins to improve the coming corn crop or to help slow the decay of corn that had been stocked for the winter months.

Individuals also use livestock fetishes for protection and fertility of horses, sheep, and cattle and hang them with prayer offerings each year. Next to livestock fetishes, puma fetishes (called **tohopko**, TOE-hope-ko) are probably the most frequently used animal fetishes among the Hopi, some as personal possessions and some reserved for clan ownership. They are used for personal well-being and protection, treatment of illness, and

Concretion

protection of the corn supply, like the tukwi. Unusual banded stones of serpentine or travertine strengthen one's natural abilities, the belief being that they make one stronger or braver.

The most important fetish for the individual, however, is the perfect ear of white corn given at the time of the naming ceremony. The ceremony takes place twenty days after birth, the first time the infant is presented to the rising sun. As in other Pueblo tribes, this ear of corn is kept for life.

Some healers use fetishes in their healing rites and may bring the actual fetishes of helpful animal spirits with them to the healing ceremonies. How the animals help varies: they may lend their strength or they may watch and protect the healer while he or she goes about the work of healing. The Hopi also use crystals imbued with special powers to divine the causes of illness. A **mahni** (MA-nee), usually a flat stone, was used in curing rites to scrape the skin/body to help remove illness. Medicine men used to wear bear claw necklaces, emphasizing the connection with the strength and healing power of the bear. Bear Clan doctors in particular have knowledge of bones, how to heal broken or dislocated bones, while Badger Clan doctors tend to focus on the use of medicinal herbs.

A number of fetishes (and other religious objects) belonging to the Hopi have been stolen and sold over the years. Many are now in the hands of private collectors who are often ignorant of the fact that Hopi religion is still practiced and that these objects are still of deep significance to the Hopi community.

THE NAVAJO

The Navajo Nation occupies a large area of land in the northeast corner of Arizona and adjacent portions of the states of New Mexico and Utah. The Navajo are an Athabaskan people who call themselves the **Diné** (din-NEH), meaning "the People," and were originally a nomadic tribe which migrated into the Pueblo Indian region from the north before the Europeans arrived. Much of their traditional religion focuses on curative ceremonies that restore health and harmony and on blessing rituals that prevent harm.

Among the Navajo there are classes of objects meant for protection from harm, those used for protection and fertility of their livestock (especially horse, cattle, sheep, goat, and pig fetishes), and those used in the restoration of harmony. If an individual has violated a Navajo taboo, whether accidentally or intentionally, that person will fall out of balance and needs to be restored to harmony. The ceremony can be long and involved as well as costly, so in certain instances the afflicted party may make an offering that represents the cause of the illness and thereby set matters right quickly and safely.

Who lies around in the sun
gray lizard
Properly
have I restored you.
In sunlight
have I dressed you.
In rainbow
have I dressed you.
In reflected sun
have I dressed you.
In the earth home you have life.
Into the earth rooms
you have re-entered.

(From Haile, NAVAJO SACRIFICIAL FIGURINES)

Navajo horse made of shell, circa 1920

Navajo kehtan made of serpentine

Certain animals, such as the bear and the ant, are among the "unappeasables." Illnesses caused by offense to these beings require the aid of a **hatathli** (ha-TATH-lee), usually translated as "medicine man" or "singer." More easily appeased animals include the turkey, weasel, dog, coyote, pig, armadillo, lizard, chicken, cat, duck, turtle, squirrel, porcupine, and beaver. The Navajo make reproduction figurines called **analne-eh** (ah-NAL-neh-eh) of these animals and include a prayer stick (**kehtan**, KAY-tawn) as part of the offering. They use a variety of materials: wood, mud, clay, or cornmeal, depending upon the animal. Stones representing various internal organs, including the brain, lungs, kidney, intestines, and liver, are sometimes added. Though there are other causes and cures, these rites and offerings may be used for a pregnant woman who has seen something stressful that may affect her unborn child.

Another type of kehtan used is the "talking" prayer stick. It is made of two approximately cylindrical pieces of wood or aragonite (usually the latter) with inlaid eyes and mouths representing male and female and wrapped in yarn. Bits of shell, turquoise, or feathers may be attached to the bundle, and occasionally one or more miniature kehtans are included. This type of prayer stick serves as protection and also ensures that prayers said when they are being held will be answered. Most singers own them, and individuals away from home or in a potentially difficult situation may carry one.

Other special charms include those for obtaining a fast horse (by invoking the speed of a hummingbird) and for luck in gambling. Another category contains ceremonial objects used to fend off evil, including those for protection when leaving the traditional boundaries of Navajoland (**Diné-tah**). They vary considerably, ranging from horned lizard fetishes for protection from dangers in the deserts to a single downy eagle plume tied to the hair or worn inside clothing close to the heart. The Navajos also use arrow points for protection. In part of a purification rite against witchcraft, the patient holds an arrowhead in the left hand and ground white shell in the right while reciting a prayer under the direction of the singer. The last category of sacred objects is **dini'schchiin** (de-NIH djish-jin), the wild game fetishes.

THE APACHE

The Apache are an Athabaskan people who call themselves **Indé** (en-DEH). Originally they were hunters, warriors, and raiders comprised of many independent bands that entered the Southwest sometime after 1200 A.D. and spread into northern Mexico by the 1500s. Today the Apache live primarily on reservations in New Mexico and Arizona.

In both raiding and hunting, it was important for the Apache to move quickly and quietly. The owl, known for its swift and silent flight, provided feathers to adorn caps. The bird could also confer protection against ghosts and both protect and warn you of evil, even evil brought by other owls. Headgear could carry other types of charms as well. A buckskin tab with a beaded four-pointed star representing the sun was sometimes used in this manner. Pendants of turquoise, abalone shell, or silver could strengthen a medicine cap. Prehistoric beads

Arrowhead

were also attached if they were one of the sacred "jewels" of the cardinal directions: white shell for the east; green or blue turquoise for the south; yellow or red argillite for the west; and black jet, shale, or steatite for the north.

A war charm, usually worn as a bandolier over the right shoulder and under the left arm, contained a variety of objects for protection. They were made of braided and twisted buckskin thongs with attachments ranging from bits of flint or obsidian, prehistoric arrowheads, various bird feathers and coral beans.

The Apache believed that these charms warded off bullets, arrows, or blows. Some also wore them at home or when traveling, for general protection.

Charm necklaces were also made for babies, with quartz crystals to protect a baby at night, cholla wood segments and corn kernels to ward off disease and bad luck, and a little red paint added to promote good health. Oriole feathers attached to the cradleboards also protected infants. Quartz crystals were used as general protective charms, to help predict the future, and to find missing objects.

Coral beans (and more recently, mescal beans) sewn into a small scrap of buckskin with a bit of the seed still visible are still worn on necklace thongs. According to traditional Apache beliefs, these seeds ward off witchcraft or will warn the wearer (by cracking) of someone nearby intending harm.

Apache arrowhead

Prehistoric arrowheads were believed to be the points with which lightning struck and as such were highly valued as charms and in curing ceremonies.

THE TOHONO O'ODHAM

The **Tohono O'odham*** (TOH-hoh-no OH-oh-tahm), meaning Desert People, live in the Sonoran Desert region of southern Arizona and northwestern Mexico. They speak a Uto-Aztecan language and are closely related to the Pima Indians who live north of them, close to present-day Phoenix. Both groups are believed to be descendants of the ancient Hohokam culture which extended from northern Mexico to north-central Arizona until about 1400 A.D.

Tohono O'odham horned lizard made of cottonwood

Objects believed to have power among the Tohono O'odham are usually owned or in the guardianship of the medicine person (**makah**, MAH-kah). Power is potentially very dangerous, and a person is dangerous when in a state of power, has gained power, or has the potential to gain power. In former days, a warrior who killed an enemy in battle or a hunter who killed an eagle had to be purified to contain the power he had achieved before he could rejoin the village. Other sources of power included journeying to the ocean to acquire salt and shells and, most importantly, dreaming. The content of a dream that brought power was never revealed lest the power be lost.

Dreams continue to be important in the Tohono O'odham community. They often reveal the capacity of the dreamer to become a makah, although few seek such a path because of the risk of the occupation. As in many other

*At one time known as the Papago

cultures, the medicine person who failed to cure or protect might be deemed the cause of the calamity and be put to death. Dreams that bring power must be thought over for a long time, even years, before the dreamer may feel ready to practice as a makah. He (or she) must remain humble and afraid of this power until it has been tested and the dreamer assured he can use it safely. For similar reasons all objects of power, such as an enemy scalp or an eagle skin, had to be sung over before they were safe to touch. Even so, these and all other related tools of a makah were kept securely wrapped in safe places, usually in caves or rocky outcroppings far from the village.

The Tohono O'odham believe that abusing animals can cause illness. Abuse includes teasing and tormenting, as well as killing game animals not needed for food. Similarly, leaving badly wounded animals or showing their spirits disrespect by leaving their bones around for dogs to chew will also cause illnesses. But these animals can also be the source of healing. A makah called to "sing away" or cleanse a patient of an animal-related illness may use a claw or image of the animal to brush or wave over the patient during the ceremony. The images are usually made of cottonwood by the makah.

Objects capable of possessing power or having important ritual use include: eagle feathers, to ceremonially brush away evil; tobacco smoke, to purify; deer tails, to help heal; and crystals or "shining stones," to find lost objects or to locate the cause of an illness or the trail of enemy warriors.

PART II

THE
ANIMALS

Navajo eagle made of Picasso marble
by Roy Davis

There are a number of animal carvings being made today that are called "fetishes," but only a handful can be truly regarded as fetishes according to the traditions of tribes in the Southwest. These include wolves, bears, coyotes, eagles, mountain lions, jaguars, bison, wildcats, snakes, and horned lizards. Livestock animals that fall into the fetish category are horses, cows, pigs, goats, and sheep. Animals such as rabbits, frogs, turtles, and owls are not. The traditional fetishes in the section that follows are indicated by the archival drawings next to the headings.

MOUNTAIN LIONS

The mountain lion, sometimes addressed as Long Tail, is generally regarded as the best and most powerful of the hunting animals. The other common name for him is puma, an Incan word. In part because the territory he covers is so great—up to a twenty-five-mile radius from the den, he is sometimes considered an appropriate fetish when traveling. At Cochiti, the medicine man uses a puma fetish for protection when traveling because it scares off danger, much as the scent of a puma scares off other animals.

At Hopi, Mountain Lion is called **Toho** (TOH-ho) and is represented as a katsina who may watch over cow, deer, pronghorn, and mountain sheep katsinas as they dance. In fetish form, he protects stored crops, homes, and the people themselves. In some Hopi villages the War Chief, who protected the villages from enemy attack in earlier times, was associated with the puma. Especially large and powerful mountain lion fetishes were owned by clans rather than

In the very earliest time,
when both people and animals
lived on earth,
a person could become an animal
if he wanted to
and an animal could become a human being.
Sometimes they were people
and sometimes they were animals
and there was no difference.
All spoke the same language.
That was the time when
words were like magic.

ESKIMO ELDER, NALUNGIAQ
(From Rasmussen,
THE NETSALIK ESKIMOS)

Above: Archival drawing,
Bureau of Ethnology, 1881

Zuni puma made of glass
by Lena Boone

It comes alive
It comes alive, alive, alive.
The lion comes alive
In the North Mountain, comes alive.
With this hunter
Will have the power to attract deer,
*   pronghorn*
Will have the power to be fortunate.

AN ACOMA SONG
(From Stirling, ORIGIN MYTHS OF
ACOMA AND OTHER RECORDS)

Navajo puma made of sugilite
by Everett Pino

Zuni puma made of sandstone
by Albenita Yunie
(NOT TO SCALE)

individuals. When an individual felt the need for the added strength of his own fetish, he usually carried it in a pouch hung around the neck. The mountain lion fetish was also used for hunting and in curing illness.

At Zuni, Mountain Lion, called **Joki-tasha** (yo-KEE tah-shah), represents the north and is the most powerful of the hunting animals. His sister is **Kuyah-palitsah** (koo-YAH pah-lit-sah), the Mother of Game and controller of all game animals. A deity named **Poshayanka** (PO-sheh-yon-kah) placed the puma in charge of the other animals of prey and gave it guardianship of the north to prevent any evil coming from that direction. Zuni hunters carry the puma fetish when hunting deer.

At the pueblo of Zia, the puma himself was believed to have the ability to will game to come to him. He also had some curative powers related to accidents, primarily hunting accidents. In Isleta, the puma is still one of five animals associated with healing.

The Keres pueblos of Acoma and Laguna call the mountain lion **sha'anyi** (shah-ANN-yih), which is also the Keres name for medicine man. Acoma hunters place puma hunting fetishes in buckskin bags containing cornmeal, turquoise, and white shell beads, with arrowheads attached. At Laguna, the fetish used when hunting the puma is the only creature that strikes faster—the snake.

Among the many Pueblo mountain lion fetishes, the Taos Indians highly prize those made from bezoar (the calcerous formation occasionally found in the stomachs of deer).

Near the Pueblo ruins of Bandelier is a prehistoric mountain lion shrine. Traditionally, Cochiti hunters sprinkled a special red ochre on the eyes of the two stone pumas, which face east, to improve their own eyesight or on the paws for strength and agility. About the time that game began to dwindle and disappear in the late 1800s, respect and ritual use of the shrine began to decline. In recent years shrine use has revived, and the stone lions are under the watchful protection of the Pueblo people in the area.

In a San Felipe ceremony, the Hunt Priest holds a spruce branch in his left hand and a puma fetish in his right. The woman who accompanies him holds corn meal in her right hand and a puma fetish in her left. In many Pueblo hunt societies, members are chosen not for their hunting

Navajo puma made of sandcast glass by Conrad House

Navajo puma made of magnetite by Roy Davis

Zuni puma made of jet by Herbert Halate

Zuni puma made of Picasso marble by Herbert Halate

*Navajo puma made of leopard stone
by Roy Davis*

*Zuni puma made of malachite
by Andres Quandelacy*

prowess but for their ability to supernaturally control game animals on behalf of the village's hunters. Although the puma was and still is most often invoked in connection with hunting at San Felipe, the head of the Scalptakers warrior society was called Mountain Lion.

Interestingly, in the Navajo creation story the Second World was inhabited by the Feline People, a tribe of tricksters constantly at war with one another. Yet, although they are recognized for their strength and skill in hunting, neither the mountain lion nor the wildcat has a significant role in Navajo cosmology.

WILDCATS

Also known as a bobcat, the wildcat is the western relative of the northern lynx. At Zuni it is the older brother to the wolf and is sometimes thought of as little brother to the mountain lion, but unlike its far-ranging relative, the bobcat usually hunts within a couple of miles of its den.

Pueblos that identify the mountain lion with deer hunting pair the wildcat with antelope hunting, although the wildcat does not actually hunt and kill anything larger than a lamb. The Hunt Chief at Isleta is called Wildcat Boy. The emergence stories of both San Juan and Isleta pueblos credit Bobcat with opening up the way from the Underworld to this one. At Zuni, in the hunting set, the wildcat is the animal of the south; its larger and rarer cousin, the jaguar, can substitute for it. Wildcat is called **Tepi-ahona** (TEH-pee ah-HO-na) in his capacity as the prey god of the south. **Tokots** (TOH-kohts),

Is the foot of the wildcat sore, oh, sore?
Are his feet so very sore?
He walks as though he were in pain.
He walks as though his old feet hurt him.

Yes, it is the old wildcat.
Truly it looks like the old wildcat.
His thighs are striped, I can see.
Yes, it is the old wildcat.

He was walking and he was walking.
He began to run down the hill at me.
But I ran right toward him
While he growled, he growled at me.

PART OF A NAVAJO CHANT
(From Schevill, BEAUTIFUL
ON THE EARTH)

Above: Archival drawing,
Bureau of Ethnology, 1881

Zuni bobcat made of Picasso marble
by Lance Cheama
(NOT TO SCALE)

*Navajo bobcat made of
mother-of-pearl by Roy Davis*

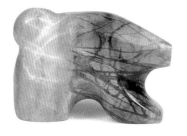

*Zuni bobcat made of Picasso marble
by Dan Poncho*

as he is called at Hopi, functions in part as a katsina who makes sure that there are enough "volunteers" to perform certain communal chores.

A Uintah-Ute story tells of Coyote giving Bobcat his distinctive appearance by mischievously shoving in Bobcat's nose and tail while the cat was sleeping. When Bobcat awoke and discovered what had happened, he went looking for Coyote, who by then was asleep himself. So Bobcat pulled Coyote's nose out into a pointy snout and yanked his tail into a bushy, disheveled thing that practically dragged on the ground.

BUSHYTAILS

This tongue-in-cheek category came about because telling a wolf from a coyote or a fox can be difficult out of context.

WOLVES

Among the Osage, the wolf is one of the seven animals used as symbols of healing, but most tribes associate it with hunting. European mythology has long vilified the wolf and created an aura of fear around it, but only in Navajo legends do we find a similar attitude of fear. Navajo witches, for example, include Skinwalkers, who have the ability to change into various animals, favoring wolves.

The grey wolf of the Greater Southwest is clearly more powerful than its cousins the coyote and the fox. Its annual hunting range is estimated at up to 1,000 or more square miles. An old Acoma tradition claimed that a runner who wore a wolf skin would never tire.

Left: Archival drawing, Bureau of Ethnology, 1881

Navajo wolf made of onyx by Jeff Davis

Natural turquoise wolf by Sarah Leekya

Zuni wolf made of Zuni stone by Francis Leekya

*Zuni wolf made of opal
by Brian Yatsattie*

*Zuni wolf made of Picasso marble
by Marnell Kucate*

Most Pueblo tribes have wolf katsinas and wolf fetishes, but the role of the wolf in their legends is small compared to that of the coyote. At Zuni, Wolf (**Yunawiko**, you-NAH-wee-koh) is ranked as the younger brother of Wildcat. His nickname there is "Hang Tail." At Isleta, the Hunt Chief carries a buckskin pouch containing a wolf fetish. In their communal rabbit hunt of previous times, the man in the lead carried a wolf fetish in his left hand.

FOXES

*Navajo fox made of opal
by Roy Davis*

Among the Apache, the grey fox is said to be useful in hunting deer. But at Hopi there is a grey fox deity to whom special offerings were given before the communal rabbit hunt in times past. Today, the skins of the **lehtaiyoh** (LEH-tai-yoh), the grey fox, and the **sikyataiyoh** (SEEK-yah-tai-yoh), the yellow fox, are used in the costumes of most katsinas.

*Navajo fox made of red abalone
by Roy Davis*

The fox katsina at Hopi is part of a class of katsina known as **wawarkatsinam** (wah-WHAR-ka-TSEE-nam), or runners, who might challenge a Hopi to a race. A race may result in a switching with a yucca whip if the runner loses against the katsina. If the runner wins, he may receive a fine basket as prize. Running was not only a practical skill in a land where a good field might be many miles from the pueblo; it remains a skill with religious implications and uses as well. In some ceremonies, runners start out on the flat-

*Navajo fox made of lepidolite
by Roy Davis*

land far to the south of their mesa-top villages and race north, hoping rain clouds will follow them.

*Navajo fox made of yellow mother-of-pearl
by Roy Davis*

Right: Archival drawing,
Bureau of Ethnology, 1881

COYOTES

Pair of Zuni coyotes made of
serpentine by Aaron Sheche

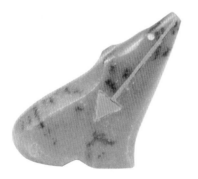

Zuni coyote made of lepidolite
by Abby Quam

Navajo coyote made of serpentine
by Jayne Quam

Our English name for the coyote comes from the Nahuatl (Aztec) language — **coyotl**. The coyote is often closely linked with the badger; in fact, the Nahuatl name for badger is **tlacoyotl** (TLA-co-yo-tul, the last syllable slurred into the one before). A number of Pueblo groups associate coyote with badger because they occasionally can be seen hunting together. The coyote's presence will often scare small animals into their dens, where the badger quickly uncovers and catches it. And if an animal is flushed out of its burrow by the furiously digging badger, the quick coyote may sometimes snatch it up.

Among some Apache groups, Coyote is credited with teaching people how to prepare and cook foods, tan hides, make moccasins, and weave various types of baskets. Furthermore, he also took credit for winning the Sun and Moon in a gambling contest and bringing them to people. In time, however, he began to steal from his human neighbors and so was banished from their camps forever.

According to the Southern Ute (or **Ningwi**), whose ancestors are thought to have migrated from California, the Ute Indians are the descendants of Ocean Woman and Coyote. At some point, Coyote left Ocean Woman and journeyed east, carrying their children in a piñon pitch-covered basket. Only the Ute were left behind.

Most other tribes usually view coyote as somewhere between a clown who stumbles over his own ego and a trickster who is a frequent nuisance. One of the most common coyote myths has to do with the placement of stars in the heavens. Coyote's curiosity, meddling, and general mischievousness disrupted the painstaking task, and the remaining stars ended up being scattered willy-nilly across the night sky. The yellow South Star is often called the Coyote Star after Coyote's yellow eyes.

In the Navajo emergence story, Coyote secretly steals the child of Water Creature, who in anger and grief at the loss begins to flood the world. During a frantic search, it is discovered that Coyote has stolen the child. The baby is recovered and returned to Water Creature, and the floodwaters recede. In another Navajo legend, Coyote has grand notions about himself, but the people object and call him simply Roamer. He objects to that name

I am the frivolous coyote —
I wander about.
I have seen Hasjesh-jin's fire —
I wander about.
I have it! I have it!

FROM THE NAVAJO CREATION STORY

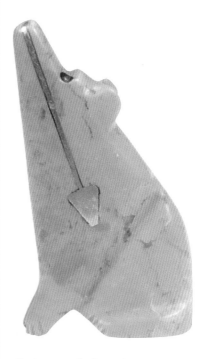

Zuni coyote made of turquoise by Todd Poncho
(NOT TO SCALE)

Zuni coyotes made of dolomite and marble by Jessie LeBouef

Zuni coyotes made of glass by Thelma Sheche

Navajo coyote made of marble by Jayne Quam

so they call him First Scolder (**Etsay Hashkeh**, et-SAY haash-KAY) instead. *He objects again, and so they call him White Coyote Howling in the Dawn.

In another story, Coyote comes to visit the Sun five times and each time angers him, causing Sun to try to kill him. But each time Sun does no more than cause Coyote to lose some fur. Sun finally takes the fur and blows it to the five directions, creating five types of coyotes: White Coyotes to roam about the Dawn (East), Blue Coyotes for the South, Yellow Coyotes for the Twilight (West), Black Coyotes for the Darkness (North), and then in the center, Grey Coyotes who must roam about all the time, living anywhere they can.

Many tribes credit the clever coyote with bringing fire to them. Among the Navajo, he stole it from the Black God and brought it to First Man and First Woman. At Zia Pueblo, the creator Thought Woman, called **Sussistinako** (soos-SEES-tee-nah-ko), gave Coyote fire. At San Juan, he retrieved fire when theirs went out. The Hopi said he tried to bring them fire, along with other important tasks, but each time he failed because he was so easily distracted, easily frightened, and extremely gullible. There is even a Navajo warn-

*The common name for coyote in Navajo is mah-ih (MAH-ee).

ing against unnecessarily harming a coyote, as the transgressor risks the curse of gullibility.

A portion of the Blessingway ceremony of the Navajo recounts the time that Coyote, as Etsay Hashkeh in this instance, argued successfully for the necessity of opposites: day and night, sun and moon, winter and summer, cold and hot, poverty and plenty, hunger and food, birth and death. At Hopi, Coyote (called **Isau'u**, ee-SAU-eu) is given similar credit, for it was he who realized the sun moved only when someone died. He told people that unless we died, there would not be enough food. He also added that when people die, they must never come back; otherwise we would not be afraid to die. He agreed to be the first to die and never come back. (In keeping with another aspect of his personality, he died from overeating.) Likewise at Zuni, Coyote is credited with setting in motion the turning of the seasons.

A Keres myth tells of the Hunt Chief instructing the animals of prey to begin preparations for a hunt by fasting for four days. But Coyote broke the fast early and was condemned to wander day and night, feeding mostly on carrion. In Jemez stories, Coyote always seems to lose out, but his status as a loser does not extend to the Coyote Clan, which is accorded an important role in religious affairs.

Zuni coyote made of rhodochrosite by Carmelia Snow

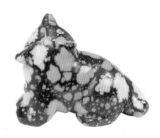

Navajo bushytail made of variscite by Roy Davis

Zuni coyote made of sodalite by Ferdinand Pablito
(NOT TO SCALE)

Not all stories regarding Coyote and hunting portray him as a buffoon either. When hunting pronghorn at Hopi, it was customary to make prayer offerings to Coyote so that he would chase the game and tire it out, making it easier to catch. Members of a Zuni hunting society are called Coyote People, and Coyote is also recognized there for his ability to tire out certain game during a long chase. One Zuni hunt ritual involves a coyote katsina that mimics the hunting and killing of a deer in order to demonstrate the proper ritual to be observed after a kill. In the Zuni ranking of the prey animals, the coyote (**suskih**, SUS-keeh) is the younger brother of the puma and older brother of the wildcat. Blue Coyote of the West is the chief of the coyotes, invoked when hunting bighorn sheep.

The Tohono O'odham say that Coyote was once a powerful medicine person. He not only scattered the stars in the sky, but he spread mesquite and saguaro cactus seeds, having obtained the seeds from Turtle.

Among many Yuman tribes* (more recently designated as the **Pai**), it was said that a bug gave Coyote the power to cure illness. Along with Buzzard and Horned Owl, Coyote was one of the animals that a Yuman shaman called upon for assistance in healing.

Coyote's frequent and distinctive howl does not go without comment. At Laguna, the coyote's howl is said to bring snow in winter and forecast rain in summer or just general changes in the weather. At Taos and San Juan, the coyote is said to howl a warning of approaching enemies. A Taos legend claims that he also led the bison into their plaza by his singing. Further, his howl is a sign that a hunter will catch a deer. An ethnologist working at the pueblo of Nambé in the early 1900s recorded a belief that the coyote's howl will bring the news of the end of the world.

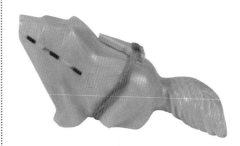

Zuni coyote made of serpentine by Florentino Martinez

The Yuman Indian groups are related by their languages and prehistoric ties of kinship. They include the Hualapai, Havasupai, Yavapai, Paipai, Diegueño, Cocopa, Mojave, Maricopa, Quechan, and Kiliwa.

There is danger when I move my feet.
I am a gray bear.
When I walk, where I step, lightning
flies from me.
Where I walk, one to be feared I am....
There is danger where I walk.

FROM A NAVAJO SONG
(Goddard, NAVAJO TEXTS)

Above: Archival drawing,
Bureau of Ethnology, 1881

Zuni bear made of jet
by Georgia Quandelacy

Zuni bear made of dolomite
by Stewart Quam
(NOT TO SCALE)

BEARS

Bears, whether the much-feared grizzly or the more common black bear, have always been accorded special regard, with many tribes giving one name for the animal in general and another sacred name for the bear spirit. Powerfully built and not easily intimidated, bears can stand on their hind legs like man, unlike any other predator. Northern Eurasian groups from Norway to Siberia commonly referred to bears by names like "Old Man of the Woods" and "Grandfather" when hunting it, both to avoid alerting the beast of their presence as well as to honor it. Many regarded killing a bear as the equivalent of killing an enemy warrior.

Despite his fearsome qualities, many tribes assigned him other attributes as well. The Oglala Sioux conceived of him as a chief of underground earth forces, in a terrifying and negative way, yet the Oglala holy man Black Elk said he obtained his knowledge of cures from the bear. And in the Ojibwa language, a young woman who had gone through puberty was said to have "become a bear."

Bears are particularly prominent in the belief system of the Navajo. **Shash** is the name for Bear, but he is usually addressed as "Reared in the Mountains" lest he think he is being called. He is regarded as the most powerful (and therefore most dangerous) of all animals. Along with Snake, Bear is a guardian of Sun's house and of Changing Woman's first hogan. It was she who gave Snake and Bear to the Navajo to protect them in their travels. But somewhere along the way, after protecting the Diné from enemies, they began to cause illnesses. In Bear's case, a ceremony was held over him and he was sent to live on Black Mountain, where his descendants can be found today.

The bear, like the coyote and the ant, is an "unappeasable" animal, so special care must be taken not to offend or show disrespect since righting the wrong is a difficult and uncertain task. Traditional Navajo will not gather piñon nuts where a bear has been gathering them, nor will they make a cradleboard from wood of a tree where a bear has scratched himself. Naturally, bears are major figures in the Mountain Way,

Zuni bear made of turquoise by Emory Eriacho

Navajo bear of sandstone by Jeff Davis

Zuni bear cub made of stabilized turquiose by Annette Tsikewa

Zuni bear made of alabaster by Herbert Him

Zuni bear made of Zuni stone by Francis Leekya

Zuni bear made of lepidolite by Roselle Lunasee

a ceremony used to heal those who have fallen ill because they violated ritual respect for the bear. Symptoms of bear-related illness range from swollen limbs to general bad luck. Severe fright from having seen a bear is one of the ailments treated by the Shooting Way ceremony.

At the pueblo of Jemez, hunters out for other game will avoid stepping on the track of a bear or even touching the track. Sometimes the bear itself is hunted. The paws are given to the medicine men of the Flint and Fire Societies, known as the Bear Group, who use them as gloves in healing. Bear is also among the animals that hunters honor by building shrines in the mountains to ritually "send them home," sending them back to the spirit world where they may once again be reborn into this world. Bear skulls are painted red and given prayer feathers before being placed in the shrines. A hunter who killed a bear was held in the same regard as one who killed a human enemy.

In earlier days at Cochiti Pueblo, there were elaborate rituals regarding the hunting of a bear. Anyone who killed a bear, eagle, or puma was eligible to join the Warrior Society just as if he had killed a human warrior. The first man to touch the dead bear was considered to be the one who killed it, regardless of whether his arrow or bullet had brought it down. The second man who touched it became a brother to the first and rushed back to the village to announce the kill. People in the village would then join in a mock attack on the bear. The paws of the bear were given to certain medicine men, as at Jemez, with the left paw being most powerful because the people of Cochiti believe that Bear is left-handed. A bear is actually ambidextrous, favoring neither left nor right. It is probably more valued due to the fact that the left side is the heart side. As at Jemez, the bear was "sent home," with its bones being given either to the river or placed in a shrine. The meat was eaten, but the skin was treated like an enemy scalp.

Taos recognized the difference between **Kah-yeh**, a supernatural bear being, and **tsiwih** (TSEEH-weeh), the bear that roams the woods. Hunters from the pueblo may kill tsiwih for meat and hold no special ceremony before or after the hunt, although they are given the practical warning that they should shoot it twice to make sure it is dead. In keeping with the popular concept of Bear's association with healing, it is thought that a wounded bear can get roots and leaves to heal itself. A Bear Society concerned itself primarily with the well-being of warriors, but also treated people

A root of herb you will eat,
At that place it stands,
A bear said this to me.
My paw is sacred,
The herbs are everywhere.
My paw is sacred,
All things are sacred.

TETON SIOUX SONG
(From Densmore,
TETON SIOUX MUSIC)

Zuni bear made of claystone

Zuni bear made of natural turquiose
by Sarah Leekya

Zuni lapis bear by Debra Gasper

Zuni bear made of treated turquoise by Emory Eriacho

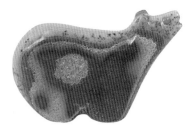

Zuni bear made of dolomite by Prudencia Quam

injured by a bear. They also held a ceremony once a year to ensure that bears would be "peaceful to the people."

At Isleta, bears were traditionally regarded as being a "people," hence the hunting of bears was forbidden and, also, of snakes and eagles. Isleta also recognized Bear's healing abilities. At Santo Domingo Pueblo, a Bear Society holds an initiation during the winter solstice. It is a warrior society whose two leaders wear bear gloves much like at some other pueblos, although there is no evidence that the gloves are used in healing rites.

At Zuni, **Ainceh** is associated with **Ku'yahpahlitsa** (ku-YAH-pah-lit-sah), the Mother of Game, and is regarded as the second most powerful animal. This is because the bear, unlike the first-ranked puma, will eat roots and berries as well as meat. This is also why he is rarely used as a hunting fetish. His shuffling gait may have given him the Zuni nick-name of "Clumsy Foot." When he appears as a kokko (spirit being) or katsina, he carries a stone axe and a tuft of wool said to represent a scalp, indicating an association with war or warriors.

The Hopi **Honau** (ho-NAH-yu), or bear katsina, is a warrior or hunter with other roles as well. Over forty years ago he appeared in a ceremony to warn of the dangers of alcohol. When asked, Bear Clan members cleanse kivas in a religious rite using a turkey vulture's wing. The Bear Clan is also the one from which the leader of most Hopi villages is usually chosen, and the members of that clan are said to sometimes have special healing powers or knowledge. The association with healing has much to do with the bear's strength, invoked against witchcraft-induced illness and to aid the mending of broken bones. White and brown bear fetishes are held by the Antelope Clan in some villages.

Among the Pueblo Indians, only the mountain lion is thought more powerful than the bear. According to a Jemez legend, when a certain deity had to punish the bear, she called upon the puma, who roped the bear with his tail.

The Jicarilla Apache of northern New Mexico associate the bear with healing but also feel that the bear, like a snake or witch, can make a person ill. Apache groups farther south credit Bear with bringing them cactus fruit, yucca fruit, piñon nuts, acorns, and berries.

Zuni bear made of serpentine by Al Lasilou

Zuni bear made of Zuni stone by Francis Leekya

Zuni bear made of serpentine by Leonard Halate

BADGERS

Zuni badger made of glass by Lena Boone

Zuni badger made of lapis lazuli by Evelena Boone

The badger is generally recognized as a rather independent animal who can mount a fierce and fearless defense when attacked. Despite this trait, he is more often associated with healing. In England, badger fat was once used to alleviate aching joints. Many tribes in the Southwest also associate Badger with some form of healing, as his digging ability is believed to qualify him as an expert on the curative properties of various roots he encounters. (During certain times of the year, the badger may even begin a new burrow each morning.)

At Hopi, where he is known as **honani** (ho-NAH-nee) and represented as a katsina, the badger is prominent in many features of village life. Badger Clan members may be sought out for healing based upon their specialized knowledge of herbs. As in old England, rheumatism is one of the ailments a Badger doctor might treat, in addition to snakebites, shock, and lightning-caused illnesses, such as partial paralysis.

The Hopi Badger Clan also controlled rabbit hunts. Before a hunt could be organized, formal permission had to be obtained from the Badger

People. Regarded as the older brother of Porcupine (another small animal who is well equipped for effective defense), Badger is sometimes linked with Coyote because a hunting coyote will occasionally follow a hunting badger in hopes of catching some small burrowing animal that the badger has flushed out but been too slow to catch. Because he spends much of his life digging underground, Badger has gained an association with planting and the purification of fields prior to planting, as well as an association with early spring and the winter solstice fire-starting ceremony. Badger often represents the south direction. Traditional stories at Hopi also link his prodigious burrowing with an ability to gain access to the spirit underworld.

At the pueblo of Zuni, Badger has similar roles. **Tonaha**, as he is called there, is known to live among the roots of cedar and juniper trees, which were traditionally used for fire-starting. In addition, his den faces south towards the winter sun. Since he does not hibernate, he can be seen outside his burrow on clear warm days in the winter, as if checking for the solstice. He is associated with the direction south, as at Hopi, and takes the

Zuni badger made of Picasso marble by Ronnie Lunasee

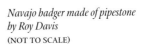

Navajo badger made of pipestone by Roy Davis
(NOT TO SCALE)

Navajo badger made of olivella shell by Roy Davis

Zuni badger made of Picasso marble by Rosella Lunasee
(NOT TO SCALE)

role of a Zuni prey god fetish with five other directional animals in a special protection set.

Although primarily connected with red, the color of the south among the Zuni, Badger is credited with giving corn its many colors. One night in the legendary past, the changing light of his fire gave corn its six colors. South is also the direction of warmth, of summer, and from whence came the knowledge of agriculture. As at Hopi, Badger controls game animals but here is restricted to small game and underground animals—with the exception of rabbits, over which the eagle has control. For a web of inter-related reasons (his involvement with fire, winter solstice observances, burrowing, farming, and the healing shared to some extent by all prey god fetishes), Badger and Badger Clan responsibilities at Zuni range from the cleaning of the bread ovens to a role in a ritual ensuring good childbirth. Badger, known as **Tonashi**, is also connected with childbirth at the pueblo of Isleta, where a badger paw was once used by midwives to help speed delivery.

In yet another tribute to the badger's digging ability, the Acoma emergence story explains that to reach this world, two sisters, the Twin Mothers of humankind, planted a pine tree that grew up from the Underworld into the Fourth World. But the hole it made when it pierced the sky was not large enough to admit passage. So Badger climbed up, enlarged it, and then came back down to allow the sisters to pass through first. For this assistance, he was permitted to be the first to enter the Fourth World after them. In a reversal of his associations at nearby Zuni, Acoma traditions associate Badger with winter and cold-weather powers. He can call up snow, a vital source of moisture. At Jemez Pueblo, Badger is rarely mentioned in traditional stories or ceremonies, probably because badgers generally do not live in the higher elevations that once comprised most Jemez land.

Badger's attributes vary widely. There was a time, according to an early ethnologist, when Navajo war leaders put ear wax from a badger or coyote in their ears or under their eyes to help improve their hearing and to see into the future. **Nah'ahtsidi** (nah-AHT-see-dee), as he is called in Navajo, is mentioned fifth in a list of hunting animals in the ceremony called the Bead Chant. The chant describes him as having a spotted body of many colors, not entirely unlike his association at

Zuni badger made of selenite by Lena Boone

Santa Clara badger made of alabaster by Mike Romero

Zuni badger made of Picasso marble by Ronnie Lunasee

Zuni with many-colored corn. Badger is said to come from the emergence place in the north and is considered very powerful because as he entered the Fourth World, he came into contact with both sky and earth. Another Navajo ceremony, in fact, refers to him as a child of the sky.

The Tohono O'odham include the badger among the animals that should never be harmed or molested. One of their legends recounts a powerful wind and devastating flood that came out of a badger hole. The Yaqui Indians of southern Arizona and Sonora, Mexico, tell the story of a time when the sun first appeared and yet no one could say what it was or even if it was male or female. Badger alone named the sun and correctly identified him as male.

SHREWS
(*Moles*)

The so-called mole fetish in fact represents a shrew, for there are no moles native to the Desert Southwest. The shrew is well suited for its role as the prey animal of the nadir or lower regions. This tiny, toothy animal is voracious, eating three-quarters of its body weight in food every day. It consumes primarily insects, but also eats earth-worms and will even kill and eat small mice. The shrew is commonly known as **kyalutsi** (k'YAH-loot-see) in the Zuni language. As a prey god, it is in charge of all small game not otherwise assigned to the other prey animals. He is also the animal of the nadir for the Tewa.

Zuni shrew made of marble by Abby Quam

Navajo shrew made of marble by Jayne Quam. Attached to its back are the other five prey guardian animals of the Zuni six directions.

Zuni shrew made of stabilized turquoise by Jayne Quam

> *From above descended powerful winged birds.*
> *Their own feathers did they pull out*
> *And with them whipped and scattered*
> *some of the sickness.*
> *All gone they thought it.*
>
> TOHONO O'ODHAM SONG
> (From Underhill, SINGING
> FOR POWER)

Above: Archival drawing,
Bureau of Ethnology, 1881

BIRDS

Bird feathers are used in a wide range of prayer offerings and are part of most healing rituals. Both the feathers and the birds themselves have other uses and roles, as well. Among the Tohono O'odham, the killing of an eagle, like the killing of a human enemy, was a chance to dream for power. Additionally, by direction of the legendary Elder Brother, some feathers were designated for fletching arrows, while others had the power to help bring rain. The outermost wing feathers were reserved for religious use by the medicine men.

Zuni quail made of Picasso marble
by Vivella Cheama

Zuni magpie made of Picasso marble
by Elroy Pablito

EAGLES

The bald eagle is recognized by the Taos Indians as brave and powerful. Generally found near areas of plentiful fish, it is primarily the Rio Grande pueblos that gave him such names as Cloud Eagle, Chieftain Bird, and Snow Eagle. At Zuni, its white feathers with black tips were highly prized, but since the bald eagle was not often present in large numbers at Zuni, the lighter-colored wing and tail feathers of juvenile golden eagles were generally used.

The downy feathers are sometimes called "breath feathers." Being so exceptionally light, they respond to the barest breath of air and have come to symbolize life in many contexts. Due to their whiteness and ability to float, they are also closely associated with clouds.

The longest feathers are also important for such vital purposes as giving medicine, purifying, blessing, and praying. At Zuni and Acoma, bear healers use eagle feathers in curing rites. Navajo healers may use the hollow quill of an eagle wing feather to suck out witchery. A Navajo antidote to witchcraft is the ground gall of an eagle mixed with cornmeal. Tohono O'odham healers use their feathers to brush away evil. Among the Yuman tribes, eagle feathers were full of dangerous power

Eagle
when he alights
there is a sound of thunder.

TOHONO O'ODHAM SONG
(From Underhill, SINGING
FOR POWER)

Zuni hawk/eagle made of Picasso marble by Elfina Hustito

Zuni eagle made of antler by Herbert Hustito

*Santa Clara eagle made of alabaster
by Mike Romero*

*Zuni eagle made of glass
by Elroy Pablito*

*Zuni eagle made of flourite
by Lena Boone*

that had to be removed by a shaman before the feathers could be safely handled.

Eagle feathers were so vital to many ceremonies at Hopi that they periodically held eagle-hunting trips to capture newly hatched eaglets from their nests. The fledglings were then tied to small cradleboards like human infants. Once home, they continued to be treated like babies and were baptized in a naming ceremony and given gifts. Raised in cages or on perches on the rooftops, they were eventually killed by smothering in sacred corn meal and the feathers removed. In traditional Hopi thought, however, they were "sent home," for it was felt that if they were treated respectfully in death, they would return from the spirit world and be reborn, just as game animals who are treated with respect will also be reborn. The number of eagles taken in this manner was small in proportion to the entire eagle population, allowing eagles to survive over the centuries.

At Hopi, it was observed that eagles could kill a snake without being harmed. When the snake struck, it generally harmlessly hit the bird's wing feathers rather than its body. During the biennial Hopi Snake Dance, when the serpent messengers are carried around the plaza in the ceremony, eagle feathers are used to distract the snakes from striking their holders.

Because he is a powerful flier able to disappear into the clouds, the Hopi **Kwahu** (eagle katsina dancer) wears a "moisture tablet" on his back to symbolize his affinity for clouds and consequent ability to bring rain-laden clouds.

Though most other groups regarded the mountain lion as the most powerful hunter, at Acoma the Hunt Chief was of the Eagle Clan, not the Mountain Lion Clan.

Serpentine eagle by Lorandina Sheche

Zuni eagle made of Picasso marble by Lorandina Sheche

Hawk
when he perches
there is a flashing of lightning.

TOHONO O'ODHAM SONG
(From Underhill, SINGING FOR
POWER)

Santa Clara hawk made of alabaster
by Mike Romero

HAWKS & FALCONS

The American kestrel, formerly known as the sparrow hawk, is a skilled hunter. Hence its facial markings, a pair of stunning dark vertical lines under each eye, inspired the warrior marks used on the costumes of Hopi hunter and warrior katsinas. This smallest of hawks is called **kele** (KEH-leh) by the Hopi and is sometimes associated with initiates in ceremonies, who are even referred to as kele. Hawks and falcons in general also have farming associations, because they eat or drive away birds and rodents that damage crops.

PARROTS

The Pueblo Indians have valued brightly colored parrot feathers highly for nearly a thousand years. Macaws, especially the fiery scarlet macaw from the jungles of Mexico, were traded as far north as the present-day Four Corners region. Not surprisingly, the bird and its bright red feathers are associated with the south and with the sun. Hopi katsinas associated with the sun and religious rituals marking the solstice wear parrot feathers, and there is a **kyash** (k'YASH), or parrot katsina. Hopi pottery from the ruin of Sikyatki often features parrot motifs, as does pottery from many other ancient Pueblo ruins. At Hopi, the more recently introduced peacock is also said to belong to the sun, for the plumage of both birds embraces a rainbow range of colors, further tying them symbolically to the sun, as rainbows are the product of rain and sunlight. At Acoma, Jemez, and several Keresan-speaking villages, the parrot is also associated with the War Societies.

Zuni parrot made of yellow mother-of-pearl by Randy Lucio

Zuni parrot made of fossilized ivory by Pernell Laate

*Zuni turkey made of mother-of-pearl
by Carlos Tsattie*

*Zuni turkey made of pipestone
by Todd Lowsayatee*

TURKEYS

Turkeys seem to have been used for both meat and feathers. Wild turkeys were hunted for food, while other turkeys were penned and apparently raised for their feathers. Their uses ranged from prayer offerings (still very important to the Hopi) to feather cloaks. The cloaks were made by twisting the feathers around cords of yucca fiber and then weaving the cords into blankets and cloaks, a fashion that largely replaced the earlier rabbit cord weavings. Among the Zuni there was a custom of leaving turkey feathers in anthills when traveling, perhaps in keeping with their use in prayer offerings and the connection of ants with travel (they seem to be everywhere one goes).

Turkeys are often closely associated with people. A part of the Hopi emergence story tells of a world flooded in order to destroy the witches who inhabited it, along with the people. To escape both flood and witches, the people fled up a reed into the next world. The turkey was the last to ascend and the foaming floodwaters touched his tail, giving it the white band. In a Navajo legend, the hero travels down a river and into a lake inside a hollow log. During his journey he is kept company by his pet turkey. A Cinderella-like folktale from the Rio Grande pueblos tells of a poor young maiden befriended by the flock of turkeys she tended. During the course of the story, her turkey friends magically provide her with beautiful clothes and jewelry to wear to a village dance. Possibly in recognition of the affinity wild turkeys have for corn, an Apache story tells how the turkey brought corn, shaking the various colored corn kernels out of his feathers.

Zuni turkey made of Picasso marble by Todd Lowsayate
(NOT TO SCALE)

Zuni owl made of Picasso marble by Arvella Cheama

OWLS

Although owls often warn of impending danger, they are not village or house protectors according to the Pueblo Indians. Most tribes regard the presence of an owl as a bad omen. Owls and witches are closely associated among a number of tribes, but owls themselves are not always characterized as malevolent beings, rather as neutral messengers of generally bad omens. The owl could warn of an attack from raiding Navajos or he could lead a Zuni war party to the Navajo, but he could also warn the Navajo of the impending attack. At Zuni, a hunter might use an owl feather to help him hunt as quietly and successfully as an owl.

Traditional Apache and Navajo also view the owl with some ambivalence. To hear an owl means an encounter with the ghost of a deceased relative, which could cause one to fall ill. However, owl-feather caps were worn to enable Apache warriors to move silently and swiftly. The Navajo Twin War Gods rid the world of a number of monsters, including Kicking Monster. His wife and children were spared death and turned into owls. In another story, however, one of the Twins, forced to remain on his own for four nights after a ceremony, was covered and protected by an who owl placed her wing over him.

The Owl katsina (**Mongwa**) of the Hopi has the responsibility of disciplining the clowns when they get completely out of hand near the end of a katsina ceremony. Hopi children were once warned that if they strayed out of doors after dark, an owl might abduct them. But at Zuni, a folk tradition holds that an owl feather placed next to an infant will help it sleep during the day. The Zuni explain the owl's uniqueness as a night bird in a story about a gambling contest in which Owl sided with the animals instead of his fellow birds. The animals lost and Owl became an outcast from all other birds, sentenced to become a night creature. Interestingly, Squirrel sided with the birds against the animals, but since he was on the winning side, he did not suffer any sanctions. Because the owl is active at night, his feathers are rarely used in prayer offerings, most of which directly or indirectly involve the sun.

The ground or burrowing owl is quite different from other owls, beginning with its habit of making its home in burrows, usually old prairie dog burrows. This comical-looking but solemn-acting little bird is called "the Priest of the Prairie Dogs" by

Zuni owl made of antler by Max Laate

Zuni owl made of stabilized turquoise by Christine Banteah

the Zuni. In times past, the Pueblo Indians grew a wide variety of corn, including dent corn and flint corn. A fragment of a Zuni story says that the owl made some of the corn softer by pecking at it.

The Hopi believe that the great horned owl helps bring hot weather and associate him with good peach crops. The practical background is the owl's habit of perching in the peach trees in that largely treeless landscape. The peaches attract his prey and the owl in turn reduces the number of pests that can harm the Hopi farmer's crop.

"Owl Meeters" is the Tohono O'odham name for the medicine men who met with the spirits of dead tribal members who took the body of an owl when they needed to bring news back to their homeland. The Tohono O'odham believed that the spirits of their warriors would warn the medicine men of the whereabouts of enemy warriors. The Maricopa Indians of central Arizona believed that dreaming of a dead relative could cause "soul loss" illness. Only a healer who had dreamed of the horned owl could effect a cure for this malady.

WATER BIRDS

A crane or heron is known as a rainbird among some Rio Grande pueblos. Ancient kiva murals often have images of white cranes, and many pueblos once had Crane Clans. A writer in the 1850s observed that when the cranes descended in huge numbers to glean the fields after the harvest, the Indians did not disturb them. This may be due in part to their association with the movement of the sun and the changing seasons, for cranes migrate north in spring during planting season and fly south in fall during the harvest.

At Zuni it is believed that the spirits of those who have died return to the Underworld in the form of ducks and that the spirits of the kokko, returning from visits to Zuni, also adopt this appearance.

The mallard, with its blue-green color, is highly prized. Like turquoise, its colors evoke both sky and water. While many birds have an association with the land and sky and by extension with the clouds and the moisture they bear, the association is strongest with the duck. All the Rio Grande pueblos and Zuni have ceremonies that involve the duck or a duck katsina. The Hopi, in their largely arid land, recognized sixteen different species of duck, according to an early twentieth-century naturalist who recorded the names.

Our great-grandfather duck came
out a short time since
From the old village by the mountains.
You have reached it; ascend the ladder
You will enter it; and here you will sit down
Hasten and enter; hasten and stand
Inside you will see your fathers all seated
Calling for seeds.

> ZUNI STORY-POEM
> (From Tedlock,
> FINDING THE CENTER)

Zuni duck made of Picasso marble
by Eugene Bowekaty

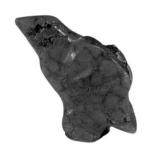

Zuni bird made of natural turquoise by Sarah Leekya

Zuni crow made of black marble by Tim Lementino

Zuni raven made of black marble by Calvert Bowannie

CROWS & RAVENS

The feathers of crows and their larger kin, ravens, are generally associated with witchcraft (as owl feathers often are). The Zuni do not use either feather on prayer sticks because crows and ravens eat carrion, but they do use them on certain kokko masks and ruffs of masks.

At Zuni, the name for crow is **kalashi** (kah-LAS-shee) and for raven is **kotollo-ah** (ko-TOL-lo-ah). For religious purposes, however, the two birds share a single name, **Kokko qu'inna** (K'EEN-na). In this context their feathers are interchangeable, and both also have an association with dark rain clouds. In keeping with the birds' unpredictable nature, however, they can either bring clouds or drive them away. Crow is said to warn of attack. The Navajo also view Crow as a messenger and a gossip, but generally Navajo legend characterizes him as allied with the malicious Turkey Vulture and Owl. Similarly, Cochiti traditions associate crows with witches and as omens of drought.

TURKEY VULTURES (Buzzards)

At Taos, they believed the vulture helped to recover slain warriors and hence used his feathers for fletching on their arrows. Taos also had a vulture katsina who appeared during times of sickness to bless and purify. Among a number of Pueblo peoples, the vulture's feathers are part of purification rituals, most of which involve ash or smoke.

Among the Tohono O'odham, the vulture **Nuwi** (NEW-wee) helped create the rivers and arroyos of their arid land with his wingtip. The Maricopa identified Buzzard* as one of the beings whom a shaman might call upon to help in a cure. To dream of Buzzard was a sign that one had been given the power to effect cures. The Navajo tell of a time when Turkey Vulture, **Djeh-koh** (d'YEH-ko), was in charge of evil and sent Crow out to seek human flesh. The Twin War Gods deterred his attempts to kill them. The vulture began to suffer from itchy skin, scratching his head until it became bald and red, a condition he still suffers from today. Navajo medicine men use his burnt feathers in ceremonies to heal those troubled by enemy ghosts.

Zuni vulture made of jet by Derrick Kaamasee

Zuni vulture made of antler by Derrick Kaamasee

Vultures are often, albeit incorrectly, referred to as buzzards.

Zuni bird made by Saul Yuselow

Zuni roadrunner made of serpentine by Benny Bacy

Zuni bird made of serpentine by Mary Peina

SMALLER BIRDS

Not all birds in Indian legend and use were large or powerful. Sometimes the smaller birds played important roles. The small but feisty shrike was strong and persistent enough to find the entrance into the next world, according to Hopi legend. In other Pueblo emergence stories, it's the swallow that finds the entrance into the next world. Swallows are associated with summer rains since their desert residence coincides with the summer rainy season. Many songbirds are also associated with rain because they come out in noisy abundance just before and after rain showers.

The horned lark is one of the few birds killed for food in significant numbers. They are primarily hunted by the Zuni, who once used horsehair snares to catch them. The people of Acoma also hunted them at one time. The hunting usually took place during winter when there was more time for trapping birds and need was greatest.

Anything done the reverse of normal could be associated with war, which was regarded as the reverse of normal activities of life. Hence, the feathers of the nuthatch are worn by the Zuni warrior kokko **Salimobia** (sa-lee-MO-bee-ah), because nuthatches often perch upside down on tree trunks. Likewise, the Salimobia society members enter and leave a kiva upside down, like the nuthatch.

The canyon wren has a remarkably loud voice for its size, and in the acoustics of a canyon it can be difficult to locate its whereabouts. Hence, he was associated with the village criers and war party leaders. Rock wrens, by contrast, are felt to be so unpredictable and "crazy" that to touch one is to risk becoming as crazy as the bird itself, according to the Zuni, whose traditions also say that witches use the rock wren's feathers.

Jays were also associated with warrior activity, as they can be startlingly aggressive and fearless, banding together to chase off hawks, eagles, and owls. Because of its blue color, the jay, like the bluebird of the Hopi, is generally associated with the direction west.

Mockingbird taught the Hopi their songs in the Underworld and divided languages among the people. He is such a constant chatterer that he can be a boon or a bane to hunter and warrior alike, telling them of their quarry's whereabouts or vice versa. The Tohono O'odham gave Mockingbird speeches to help bring rain, because they believed the bird to

Zuni bird made of rock crystal by Leland Boone

Zuni roadrunner made of Picasso marble by Fabian Tsethlikai

Zuni bird made of Zuni stone by Sarah Leekya

Zuni woodpecker made of Picasso marble by Robert Halusewa

be the most eloquent of speakers, able to "stretch his words like ropes between the mountains."

Because the roadrunner track is shaped like an X, making it difficult to tell which way the bird is headed, roadrunner feathers were sometimes used at Zuni in war-related rituals in the hope that the enemy would be similarly confused as to the whereabouts of their warriors. The roadrunner's strength and aggressiveness (it will battle a rattlesnake) give it a role in some Zuni curing rites. A member of the Roadrunner Clan, for example, treats rheumatism or illnesses that cause convulsions. When a member of the village died at Isleta Pueblo, a circle of roadrunner tracks was made to prevent any evil spirits from remaining behind. The Hopi once tied the feathers of the roadrunner to the tails of their horses to make them swift. The roadrunner is still represented as a katsina there.

A Yaqui legend says that the blackbird stole corn from the devil, who was hoarding it, and brought it to them.

HUMMINGBIRDS

The jewel-like beauty, blazing speed, and aggressive nature of this diminutive bird has earned it a place in the myths and rituals of many Southwest Indian tribes. Among the Navajo, for example, he could be used to obtain a fast horse. The custom was to use a live hummingbird to rub down a turquoise horse fetish which was then placed in a pouch and tied around the neck of a mare about to foal. After birth, the new-born colt was rubbed with the fetish pouch as a final blessing and prayer for speed.

In Tohono O'odham legend, the hummingbird **Wipismal** (WEE-pees-mal) succeeded in finding where Wind and his friend Rain had been hiding for four years, after Bear, Coyote, and Buzzard had failed at the task. Hummingbird performs the same task in a story from Cochiti Pueblo. The Hopi tell a story of a young brother and sister accidentally left behind during a great famine and drought. The boy made his sister a hummingbird from the pith of a dry sunflower stalk. As the little girl played with it, Spider Woman made it into a real bird who then brought the two children food and saved them.

Zuni hummingbird made of yellow mother-of-pearl by Carlos Tsattie

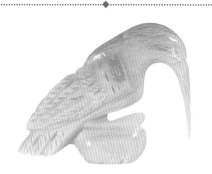

Zuni hummingbird made of yellow mother-of-pearl by Randy Lucio

Among the Apache, the hummingbird symbolized fertility and was also an important part of their creation story. This tiny bird led the Apache into the upper worlds and was a messenger between the Apache and various supernatural beings. At one time the hummingbird was used on shields by Apache warriors who hoped to be able to move as quickly and be as difficult to see in motion.

The speed of the hummingbird is also recognized at Zuni, where a racer takes seeing a hummingbird as a good omen. At both Acoma and Zuni, he has roles as a scout and messenger. Acoma recognizes two types of hummingbirds: the sun bird (the broadtail hummingbird) and the flower bird (the rufous hummingbird). The feathers have some religious use, but its main importance is as a pollinator. An Acoma story tells how the hummingbird received his iridescent colors by flying through a rainbow. At Hopi, **Tocha** (TOH-cha) is recognized as a katsina.

TWO HORNS

The category of Two Horns includes not only deer, pronghorn, bison, bighorn sheep, and elk, but also the rabbit, for reasons explained below.

DEER

Deer is generally the first big-game animal killed by hunters in the United States and is certainly the most widely hunted. Deer antlers are thus the most visible trophy and symbol of hunting. Among many tribes in the Southwest, the deer is also the most important big-game animal. For most, there is an interesting relationship between deer and crops and between hunting and farming. The Tohono O'odham, for example, have a story about **Huawi** (h'WAH-wee), Mule Deer, instructing people to plant and grow food and to stop hunting deer so much.

At the Keres pueblo of Zia, the deer is the animal of the north. At the Keres pueblo of Cochiti, the **Heluta** (he-LOO-ta) katsina, spiritual father of all katsinas, brings deer which he has raised "like corn," according to one translation. In another legend, Deer tells the people that his dewclaws are his seed.

Our elder brother deer
Our elder sister deer,
We are going to meet you
We are going to meet you.

Then deer will come
Then deer will come.
Come on with us
Come on with us.

Now you follow us
Now you follow us.
Here we are dancing
Here we are dancing,
In this manner
In this manner.

TEWA SONG
(From Spinden,
SONGS OF THE TEWA)

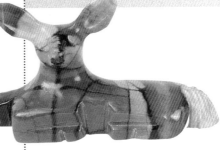

Zuni deer made of Picasso marble by Fabian Tsethlikai

*Zuni deer made of antler
by Pernell Laate*

*Zuni deer made of mother-of-pearl
by Andres Quandelacy*

"Whenever you kill a deer, do not throw these away because they are my seed."* At Cochiti and other Rio Grande area pueblos, deer bones were traditionally buried in the cornfields. They reasoned that since fawns grow into young deer in the short period of three months, the presence of deer bones could make the corn grow quickly, before drought or an early freeze could kill it.

In Taos Pueblo, deer tend to be thought of as bringers of rain or even as rain makers. At Acoma, they identify the white-tailed deer as Water Deer, recognizing that unlike the mule deer, it prefers to remain near steady sources of water. At Zuni the Rain Priest of the North, **Saiyatasha** (sai-ya-TA-sha), can bring in the deer. He is often accompanied by the deer kokko, who has a green face and wears eagle and owl feathers. Another kokko, **Sulawitsi** (sue-LAH-weet-see), usually translated as Fire God, carries a fawn skin containing seeds. **Sowi-nwa** (SO-wee-n'wah) is the name for deer at Hopi, where it is also recognized as a katsina. The Deer Clan there is affiliated with the other two-horns clans of the bison, elk, bighorn sheep, and pronghorn.

A Zuni hunter who has just killed a deer may offer the deer's last breath to his hunting fetish (a

Also from Spinden's Songs of the Tewa.

puma, which may be fed by dipping it in the deer's blood). Or he may inhale it himself, praying: "This day I give you my thanks for your rains, your seeds, and the mysteries of life which I inhale." The deer's head is then placed so it faces east, as is done for humans who have died. The hunter helps "send it home" to be reborn by digging a small hole, which represents the entrance to the spirit world, and depositing offerings of ground shell, turquoise, hematite, and corn pollen to ask it to return.

Zuni deer made of Picasso marble and fossilized ivory by Raybert Kanteena

Deer hunting can involve considerable preparation. At Zuni, bits of shell, corn meal, and pollen are scattered in the tracks to ensure a successful hunt. The Yuman Indians of the lower Colorado River region believed one should not call a deer by its name when planning a hunt lest it be alerted. Instead, they referred to a fat deer as "a beautiful woman." At Santa Ana Pueblo there were songs for locating deer, for tracking a wounded deer, for first touching a fallen deer, for skinning and butchering a deer, and for carrying it back home. The songs included references to the rain and clouds of the deer's mountain home, with the clear implication that they should follow the deer back to the village, a prayer belief shared by many Pueblo peoples.

The Navajo envisioned game animals such as

deer, elk, pronghorn, and bighorn sheep, known as **Dini** (DEH-nih), as carrying packs of corn on their backs. They were in charge of the corn-growing rite of the Fire Dance. Showing lack of respect to deer can result in illness, ranging from eye and ear problems to urinary problems. A hunter who fails to offer proper respect to his quarry will find that they have disappeared, having turned themselves into a dead tree, a bush, or even a rock. Once successful, a hunter must properly dispose of the deer bones and sprinkle them with corn meal.

PRONGHORN

Pronghorn antelope are properly called American pronghorn, as they are not true antelope but are actually related to goats. Pronghorn are not only fleet, but far-ranging, often covering between twenty and thirty miles in a single night. The hooves were said to be made of black jet, and the beauty and strength of the pronghorn are much admired. Its fierce fighting during rutting season earned it the role of a warrior in at least one Zuni story.

At nearby Acoma, a legend tells of the rain and crops being taken away and hidden. The pronghorn found and released them from captivity. At Acoma, ceremonial treatment is an important part of hunting the animal. After the kill, its head is placed facing east, dressed in a jet necklace, fed corn meal, and generally treated with great respect so that the departed spirit will return as a new

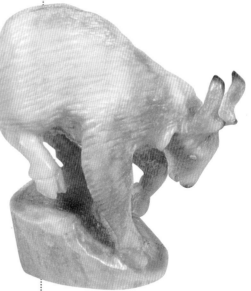

Zuni antelope made of antler by Derrick Kaamasee
(NOT TO SCALE)

pronghorn. The skull is also treated carefully, with the final step being the stringing of prayer feathers between the horns. The bobcat is the fetish used in hunting the pronghorn both at Acoma and Laguna.

At Zia Pueblo the pronghorn is the animal of the west. In the Tiwa pueblo of Isleta the War Chief, in charge of all human and animal scalps taken, wore a cap with pronghorn horns attached. The Hopi War Chief wore a similar cap. An interesting difference in the obligations of this position was that at Isleta the War Chief was not supposed to kill anything.

BISON

Commonly — if incorrectly — called buffalo, the American bison is usually thought of in connection with the Great Plains, although bison herds once extended as far west as Arizona and as far south as northern Mexico. Among many pueblos, rain belongs to the deer and snow to the bison.

The Hopi Indians still hold a **mosayru** (MOE-sigh-rue), or buffalo ceremony, early each winter to pray for winter moisture. A buffalo dance is also held at Cochiti to bring snow, during which anyone who is ill can request that the dancers perform one round of the dance in front of their home in order to "bring good medicine." Closer to the great herds of the plains, Taos Pueblo credited Coyote with bringing the bison. Associated with the winds, burning a bison skull was part of a rite against high winds, drought, and extreme cold. At Zia Pueblo the bison was the animal of the east.

The Zuni, who also hold a buffalo dance, would hunt bison whenever a herd wandered into their region. Because the animals could move on quickly and suddenly, it was important to slow them down until word could get back to the vil-

Navajo bison made of Baltic amber

Navajo bison made of alabaster by Herbert Becenti

Zuni bison made of fossil ivory by Rhoda Quam

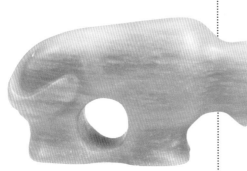

*Zuni bison made of alabaster
by Tony Chopita*
(NOT TO SCALE)

lage and hunting preparations and prayers could be made. Called "slow medicine," a sharp-pointed medicine rock was stuck down into a bison's hoofprint. Hooked devil's claw seed pods and datura plants were similarly employed.

The Buffalo People are prominently featured in a number of Navajo legends, and the bison's hide and tail are required for the making of rattles used in the Shooting Chant. Part of the chant refers to the warmth and moisture of the bison's body making plants grow and produce pollen.

BIGHORN SHEEP

Because the weasel is a high mountain predator who lives in the same alpine zone, it is used as the fetish animal by the hunters of Acoma and Laguna when hunting the bighorn or mountain sheep. Further to the southwest, the Zuni identify the coyote as the animal fetish for hunting bighorn sheep. Among the Rio Grande pueblos, the bighorn sheep dancer generally appears with the other Two Horns, as he also does at Zuni. But it is at Hopi where the bighorn sheep has the greatest significance.

The Hopi believe the bighorn sheep, along with deer and pronghorn, has power over both rain and spasms of the body. The bighorn sheep is also capable of conferring its sharp vision and hearing. To avoid alerting it during preparations for a hunt, it was referred to as a "rat." Incredibly, the preferred traditional method of hunting this hardy and agile beast was to encircle it, tire it out by chasing it on foot, and then smother it. To spill its blood in the killing was to risk a whirlwind or severe sandstorm.

Although the Hopi did hunt it, a substantial trade with the Havasupai Indians also brought the

Navajo ram made of alabaster by Roy Davis

Ram made of pipestone by Ulysses Mahkee

Navajo ram made of serpentine by Roy Davis

*Zuni ram made of fossil ivory
by Andres Quandelacy*

Hopi the horns, highly prized for a wide range of purposes, from cups to ceremonial headdresses, for an important religious society, and as tools. The horns (made of keratin) were boiled down to coat their bows, which were then wrapped with hide and coated again to strengthen them, as other tribes did with sinew. They also regarded the bighorn or mountain sheep as the best tasting game meat.

In carvings, it can be difficult to tell the difference between domesticated goats or rams and bighorn rams without knowing the intent of the artist.

ELK

The Hidatsa of the northern Great Plains associated the elk with love magic and gave it a role in the flute myths, stories of love and courtship. The connection probably came from the constant dueling between male elks over the female herd. Herds can approach some two hundred animals, and bulls may weigh up to a ton. In many areas of the Southwest, numbers of elk dwindled or completely disappeared in the nineteenth century, so that a few tribes came to regard it as simply another type of deer (which, according to its scientific classification, is quite accurate). The existing herds now abundant in Arizona and New Mexico are the result of efforts to reintroduce them.

Zuni elk made of antler by Max Laate

The Hopi do not have an elk katsina, but elk antlers are used to ceremonially close trails into the village before certain religious observances. In Zia Pueblo, the elk belongs to the Fire Society, as does the katsina **Heluta** (HE-lou-tah) who brings the deer. The elk also appears in the Zia buffalo dance. Cochiti once held an elk dance every three years, and Taos has an elk dance.

The pueblo of Nambé has an elk dance (called **Tashare**) which its people established under inter-

*Zuni elk made of antler by
Derrick Kaamasee*

esting circumstances. Many years ago, the pueblo sold some land and used the money to buy goods, including turquoise necklaces, dance blankets, and buckskins, in order to acquire the permission or rights from Taos Pueblo to hold an elk dance. Held on October 4, it is not to regenerate elk or other game, but as a rite of regeneration for the pueblo itself. They believe that as long as the elk dance is properly and regularly performed, the tiny pueblo of Nambé will not die out.

Hunters from Laguna and Acoma use a wolf fetish in hunting the elk. A Hopi story relates the difficulty in hunting such a large, wary, and powerful horned animal. The Twins had been sent to hunt the elk, but a tiny gopher warned them that the mighty elk might kill them instead. So while the elk slept, the gopher burrowed underneath it and chewed off the fur over its heart. The Twins were then able to kill it with their lightning. Once killed and the proper rites performed, the Twins realized they had forgotten their knives, so a chipmunk butchered the elk for them with his sharp teeth. And hence it was the streaking of the elk's blood that gave the chipmunk its stripes.

RABBITS

M ost Euro-American myths associate the rabbit with fertility or assign it qualities of shyness and timidity. The Winnebago Indians of the Great Lakes area, like Afro-American storytellers of the American South, saw the rabbit as a trickster, much like the coyote of Southwest Indian legends.

In prehistoric times, the rabbit of the Desert Southwest was hunted for both meat and fur, which was cut into strips and woven with yucca fiber to create rabbit-skin blankets. In historic times at Zuni, the rabbit was hunted for food, but the first rabbit taken in the hunt season had a special function. The Great Father **Koyemsi**, who leads the other nine Zuni mudhead clowns when they appear in Zuni ceremonies, would dip his hunting fetish in its blood. Afterwards, the kokko **Chakwena Okya** (choc-WIN-ah OAK-ya), Keeper of the Game and also the special guardian of women in childbirth, used the rabbit in a ritual to bring on puberty in a young woman or to increase a woman's fertility. Hence the rabbit was also associated with safe birth and long life for children.

Zuni rabbit made of antler by Max Laate

Navajo rabbit made of serpentine

Navajo rabbit made of rhodochrolite by Roy Davis

Zuni rabbit made of stabilized turquoise by Daisy Natewa

The jackrabbit (**pokya**, POK-ee-ah) at Zuni is said to have songs for snow, and the cottontail (**akshiko**, AHK-shee-ko) songs for rain. They illustrate another aspect of fertility, the importance of both winter and summer moisture in growth. In the **Mamzrau** Hopi religious observance, a figure known as Rabbit Mother is associated more generally with fertility of crops and humans, but not fertility of game. In at least one Pueblo village, Rabbit Mother was associated only with plant fertility. The **Masau'u** katsina (ma-SOW-uh), often thought of as being in charge of the Underworld, wears a robe of blood-soaked rabbit skins. While death is not generally associated with fertility in Euro-American culture, it is part of the cycle of life. Plants, for example, germinate, grow, become fertile, bear seeds, and die before new seeds can germinate and thus renew the cycle.

Jackrabbits are viewed as part of the family of Two Horns. Like deer, jackrabbits will run in a large circle when pursued by hunters. The Hopi name for jackrabbits, **so'wi**, is very close to **sow-i'nwa** (so-WE-nwah), their word for deer. As at Zuni, members of the Sacred Clown Society at Laguna and Cochiti may not eat jackrabbits. Members are also forbidden to eat the Rocky Mountain bee plant, which rabbits also nibble. Both the clown society and the jackrabbits are said to be involved with weather control and the promotion of fertility.

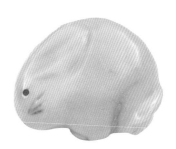

Zuni rabbit made of tagua nut by Annette Tsikewa

BEAVERS

*Zuni beaver made of jet
by Justin Red Elk*
(NOT TO SCALE)

Early Euro-American interest in the beaver seemed limited to using its pelts to make fine hats for the stylish gentlemen of Europe. Hence, there was a lively commerce between many North American tribes and the large European trading companies that established themselves in the New World in the seventeenth and eighteenth centuries.

Not all tribes, however, participated in the beaver pelt trade. Initially, the Osage were adamantly opposed to killing beaver because tribal traditions said that they were a related "people." Further east, the Cherokee had a tradition of calling on Beaver to bring strong permanent teeth for their children. The Nez Perce credited Eagle and Beaver with bringing fire.

Among the Indians of the Thompson River area of British Columbia there is a story that Beaver single-handedly stole fire from the Pine Trees, who were keeping it from all other beings. Among the Navajo, Beaver (**Tsah**) is one of the Water People, who can both cause and cure certain water-connected illnesses. He also assists the hero of a Navajo story with vital information and help. Beaver Man and Otter Woman, for example, gave the Twin War Gods their skins to keep them from freezing when their father, the Sun, tested them with bitter cold. The Apache creation story includes a mention of Beaver as the one who gave them water.

Zuni beaver made of alabaster
by Travis Panteah

Zuni beaver made of serpentine
by Wilfred Cheama

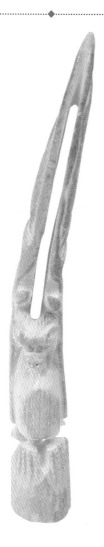

*Zuni bat made of antler
by Garrick Weeka*

BATS

There are nearly twenty species of bats found in one region or another of the American Southwest. Most feed on insects, although two feed on the nectar and pollen of cacti and agaves. The quick erratic flight of the bat inspired Apache warriors to occasionally use its image on their shields in hopes of being as difficult to hit and as silent in their approach and night travels.

Among the Navajo, **Jaa'abani** (JA-ah-bah-nee, literally "buckskin ears") the Bat is the Night Guardian of the East. In payment for his help in overcoming an enemy in Navajo legend, he was given a small yellow animal skin and so is portrayed with a small yellow diamond on his body. Another legend says that in order to gain Bat's help in a gambling contest, a young man gave him

a small buffalo skin and this is
why the bat still wears a furry
coat. The Navajo hatathli
Miguelito is recorded as saying that at
one time medicine men could talk to bats and
that bats could converse with lightning.

According to the Hail Chant, Bat Woman
helped one of the Twin War Gods who then
rewarded her with feathers that turned into all
kinds of birds. An Apache version relates that Bat
Woman was given feathers in which to cloak herself, but she failed to guard them and they were all
taken away by birds before she could apply them.

*Zuni bat made of Picasso marble
by Elfina Hustito*

Antler bat by Garrick Weeka seen from the side

Zuni porcupine made of Picasso marble by Todd Lowsayette

Zuni porcupine made of serpentine by Elfina Hustito

PORCUPINES

The porcupine, related to the squirrel and beaver, is regarded by the Hopi as being a clan relative of the badger. In one Hopi migration story, Butterfly flew about the land looking for a better place for Badger and Porcupine to live and decided that the village of Oraibi was the best. But the people of Oraibi were reluctant to share their lands with the newcomers unless they could prove their value to the community. This Badger (**Honani**) did so readily with his knowledge of plants and his ability to cure with them. Porcupine (**Muungyaw**) was able to stay after he demonstrated his ability to create a magical blue paint from piñon gum, a yellow paint from rabbitbush, and a red paint from skunkbush berries.

The Havasupai felt that, along with the hoot of an owl, the noise of a porcupine told of a relative dying somewhere. A strip of porcupine skin with the quills still attached was worn on a cap or the back of a shirt to ward off illness.

MICE

Mice rarely play a role, even in folktales. At Hopi, however, there is a story of an old badger doctor who was incensed to learn that the Mice People claimed to be doctors, too. Determined to unmask them as frauds, he took to his bed, did not eat for four days, and then summoned the mice doctors to cure him of his illness. As soon as the mice entered, they began to sing, "Four days he did not eat...." Badger was so angry at having his deception exposed that he snatched up a staff to kill the mice, but in his weakened state they all escaped. According to the story, although the mice left the village and scattered, if they find a Hopi ill or injured away from home, they will secretly doctor him until he is found or can return home on his own.

Navajo mouse made of Picasso marble by Roy Davis

Navajo mouse made of cowry shell by Roy Davis

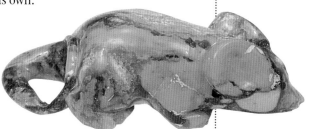

Navajo mouse made of stabilized turquoise by Roy Davis
(NOT TO SCALE)

*Zuni frog made of septarian
by Abby Quam and Clayton Panteah*

*Navajo frog made of alabaster and turquoise
by David Yazzie*

*Navajo tadpole made of
alabaster by Ron Upshaw*

FROGS &
TADPOLES

Water creatures are not only associated with water, but with the desire or prayer for water. In some pueblos, tadpoles represent the early summer rain, frogs the mid-summer rain, and dragonflies the late summer rain. In the more arid regions of the Desert Southwest, the spadefoot toad is dormant during the dry season and begins its brief, frenetic life only after a pounding summer rain. The spadefoot comes to the surface so soon after a downpour that it seems to have fallen with the rain, thereby cementing its relationship with the life-giving, renewing summer rain.

Among the Hopi there is a frog katsina, **Pakwabi** (pahk-WAH-bee), but he appears only rarely. Frog designs, however, can be found on the backs of some katsina, and tadpole designs are used on rattles, prayer offerings, dance sticks, and pottery. Some religious societies use frog carvings on their altars.

Navajo legend has it that at one time in their past men and women fought and finally separated. When the groups were reunited, both Toad and Frog assisted in a cleansing purification rite.

According to one version of the Zuni creation story, the people coming up from the dark underworld had tails, webbed feet, and webbed hands. It was not until they came into the sunlight that they assumed human form. In the Zuni story of the migrations, the newly created people were crossing a cold, red, rushing river (possibly the Colorado River), when the terrified mothers with newborn children panicked and fell into the rushing water. As the infants sank, they turned into water creatures—frogs, newts, salamanders, turtles, and toads. In the process, they also created "the way of dying and the path of the dead," for the Zuni afterworld is not underground but underwater in a lake.

One of the more sacred fetishes to the Zuni, assembled for a ceremony overseen by a rain priest, is reported to include a live frog. The frog is a frequent motif on Zuni pottery and on pottery vessels said to have been used in ceremonies. Frog carvings and shell jewelry with frog motifs are often found in archaeological excavations of prehistoric Southwest Indian sites. However, there is no traditional use of stone or shell frog fetishes at Zuni or at any of the other pueblos.

The Mohave have a traditional story which tells of Frog bringing fire to the people, as in a story also

Zuni frog made of black marble by Roselle Shack

Zuni frog made of serpentine by Ricky Laahty

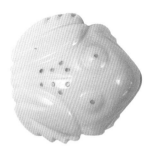

Navajo frog made of shell by Roy Davis

Zuni frog made of stabilized turquoise by Evalena Boone

Acoma frog made of alabaster

Havasupai frog made of alabaster

told by the Yaquis. In the Yaqui legend, Frog had the help of Crow, Dog, and Roadrunner. In another Yaqui story, Frog also brought rain after Blackbird and Roadrunner failed in their attempts. The Maricopa of central Arizona held a belief that someone who dreamed of Frog could bewitch people by "shooting" them with a bit of charcoal from a cremation. Such a person could also handle coals with impunity, even to the extent of walking on coals.

TURTLES

Many groups, from the Iroquois and the Seminole tribes of the Americas to the people of Thailand, believed that the world rested on the back of a turtle. The Lakota use a beaded turtle to hold the umbilical cord of newborn girls for protection and a long life. Lizards were used for those of the boys. In the Southwest, the role of the turtle is not as significant.

The Hopi sometimes address Turtle as "Little Brother" and value the turtle for its shell, which is used as a leg rattle on some katsinas. In areas where both water turtles and land turtles live, there are sometimes separate functions. At Isleta, one group uses water turtle rattles and the other land turtle rattles in their ceremonies. The Maricopa had an injunction against holding a turtle shell over a child, as it would stunt the youngster's growth.

In certain Navajo ceremonies, medicine has to be dispensed from either an abalone shell or a turtle shell; no other container is acceptable. Turtle

Zuni turtle made of mother-of-pearl by Loren Burns

Zuni turtle made of shell by Loren Burns

Zuni turtle made of tiger eye by Vivella Cheama
(NOT TO SCALE)

Long ago in the north
Lies the way of emergence!
Yonder our ancestors live,
Yonder we take our being.

Yet now we come southwards
For cloud flowers blossom here.
Here the lightning flashes,
Rainwater here is falling!

SANTA CLARA TURTLE DANCE SONG
(From Spinden, SONGS OF
THE TEWA)

Zuni turtle made of black marble by
Chris Yuselew

Zuni turtle made of Ojo rock
by Leroy Chavez

shell can also be substituted for flint as armor against lightning. In several versions of the story of the Beauty Way ceremony, Frog Man and Turtle Man are the two warriors who lead a scalping raid on the Pueblos. Together they survive attempts to kill them with by ax, by fire, by boiling, and by drowning.

Like frogs and tadpoles, turtles are not traditionally used as fetishes by the Pueblo tribes.

SNAKES & WATER SERPENTS

The serpent is an important entity in the ancient cultures of Mexico. The Feathered Serpent of the Aztec and Maya, known respectively as **Quetzalcoatl** (ketts-tzeh-KWA-tle) and **Kukulcan** (coo-cool-CAHN), appears to have influenced cultures to the north, from the prehistoric Pueblo Indians of the Southwest to the Hopewell cultures of the Mississippi River Valley. In some instances, the feathered serpent figure evolved into a water serpent but still retained many of the fearsome qualities of the Feathered Serpent.

The fierce nature of Quetzalcoatl seems to be reflected in a number of Pueblo stories about the water serpent. At Pecos Pueblo, he was a dangerous figure who threatened to destroy the village when they refused his demands for sacrifices. Eventually they overcame him, but not before his thrashing tail cut deep arroyos into the surrounding countryside. A Zuni story tells of the time that **Kolowisi** (ko-lo-WEE-see), as they call the water serpent, began to flood the world because the people had strayed from the traditional path. The Zuni fled to

Storm Serpent Old Man,
Come hither now
For here we are dancing.
Laden with rain
Now you arrive!

TEWA SONG
(From Spinden, SONGS OF THE TEWA)

Zuni snake made of abalone
by Kenny Chavez

Zuni onyx snake by Eugene Bowekaty

Zuni rattlesnake made of marble
by Kenny Panteah

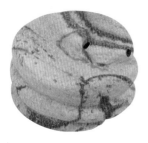

Zuni rattlesnake made of mother-of-pearl by Kent Pantech
(NOT TO SCALE)

Navajo snake made of sandstone by Roy Davis

the top of a nearby mountain, but even there they were not safe. It was not until a young boy and girl, dressed in their finest clothes and jewelry, walked out into the great sea of water and sank from sight, that the floods subsided. The Hopi have a similar story, but the pueblo involved was destroyed and the survivors (who had maintained the old ways) moved north without a sacrifice. A Tohono O'odham legend about **Nehbig** (NEH-big), the water serpent, tells how it began to flood the world because of an offense against it. It demanded and received a sacrifice, as at Zuni.

The water serpent also has an association with corn among groups ranging from the Hopi of northern Arizona to the Cora Indians of western Mexico, where he has a relationship with the Corn Mothers. Among the Seri Indians who live along the desert coast of the Sea of Cortéz (Gulf of California) north of the Cora, crushed and ground snake bones were once used in healing rituals.

The speed and suddenness with which snakes can strike give them an association with lightning in many cultures. Because lightning is generally associated with rain, snakes often share that connection as well. Among the Tewa groups, the Water Serpent **Avanyu** (AH-van-yu) is depicted as a snake with cloud symbols above his back and head and with lightning issuing from his open mouth.

Palolonkon (pa-lo-LON-kon), as the Hopi call him, is associated both with the water that flows unseen under the earth and with the springs where the water seeps out. He is represented by a katsina and honored at a water serpent ceremony held in winter. A preliminary planting of corn in the kiva is a part of that religious observance. The famous Hopi Snake Dance, which has received overwhelming attention from non-Hopi, involves the use of snakes as messengers to carry prayers for rain. The entrance holes to the underground dens of snakes are believed to be symbolic entrances to the Spirit World.

At Zuni the horned water serpent (Kolowisi) appears during an initiation ceremony, and his image sometimes appears on Zuni pottery. He is regarded as the most powerful fetish animal, though the fetish, carved of antler, is traditionally

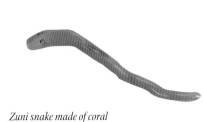

Zuni snake made of coral by Eugene Mahooti

Zuni snake made of shell by Willard Laate

Zuni water serpent made of antler by Edna Leki
(NOT TO SCALE)

Navajo snake made of coprolite by Roy Davis

Zuni snake made of Picasso marble by Michael Coble
(NOT TO SCALE)

attached to a fetish bowl or used in a larger rite, where it belongs not to an individual but to a religious society.

In the Navajo Beautyway ceremony, a sandpainting image of Endless Snake or Big Snake With No End, **Klish-tso-nuhtih** (klish-TSO-nuh-teh), is used to treat people who have been bitten by a snake or who have nightmares about snakes. A diamond design is placed on the forehead of white and yellow male snakes to represent their power. Blue and black female snakes have yellow diamonds of pollen to symbolize their power. Red tongues indicate the snake is dangerous or poisonous. Snake-related curing ceremonies treat people who have certain types of body sores, kidney trouble, or pains in the spine. The afflictions can arise from drinking water that a snake has swum through or sitting near a place where lightning has struck.

Among the Havasupai of the Grand Canyon area, if a snake entered a house, its presence foretold illness, injury, or even death for a member of the household or a close relative. A man whose wife was pregnant was not allowed to kill a snake under any circumstances lest the baby be born with weak limbs.

A Tohono O'odham folk tale, echoing a similar tale from the Maricopa, tells about the time when Rattlesnake was still a harmless creature and was tormented by children who broke out his teeth and teased him mercilessly. He complained bitterly to First Born who gave him fangs and poison to protect himself, along with a rattle to warn the children and other creatures away. The price for this defense, however, was a life of solitary travel without friends.

Snake fetishes were used at Laguna when hunting the puma. A few pueblos once used a snake fetish with an arrowhead attached to help the archer shoot quickly, accurately, and successfully.

Navajo snake made of stabilized turquoise by Jake Livingston

Navajo snake made of mother-of-pearl by Livingston family

Zuni snake made of serpentine by Nelson Yatsattie

OTHER REPTILES

Zuni lizard made of chrysocol by Pernell Laate

Zuni lizard made of Picasso marble by Staley Natewa

Many Indian groups associate both reptiles and amphibians with skin ailments. Interestingly, in English both a skin ailment, herpes, and the study of reptiles and amphibians, herpetology, are connected by the same word root.

Of all the members of the lizard family, the horned lizard (commonly and mistakenly referred to as a horned toad) appears especially frequently in southwestern Indian belief systems. The Tohono O'odham call it **chemamagi** (che-MA-ma-gee) and maintain that it can cause a range of ailments if molested. By the same token, it can help cure or even prevent those same problems. In some instances, a carved wooden image of the horned lizard was used. Painted with red hematite, it was usually made of wood struck by lightning. Some of the Yuman tribes believed that a shaman who dreamed of a horned lizard could cure "soul loss," which came from dreaming of a dead relative.

Among the Navajo, the horned lizard can cause any number of illnesses, but he can also help treat others. Because he eats ants (up to thousands in a single month), ant-caused illness is often treated

Zuni horned lizard made of yellow mother-of-pearl by Todd Estate

using water in which a horned lizard has been dipped. His body "armor" also gave rise to the belief that he is immune to harm from lightning or thunder. For this reason, corn pollen that has been shaken on a baby horned lizard provides protection against lightning. According to custom, this same corn pollen can be applied to a woman in labor. Several species of horned lizards are not egg-layers but give birth to live young, hence its connection to childbirth. The vigor of the newborn horned lizard may also explain why some Navajo will use a live horned lizard in the infant blessing ceremony. On occasion, a horned lizard fetish may be prescribed for someone who is about to leave Navajoland and live in the more southern deserts or who has suffered some illness while living there.

Among the Hopi, the **manangyue** (ma-NONG-yeh) is represented as a katsina. At one time, Hopi youths hoping to speak to a young woman were advised to ask the assistance of this blue-streaked lizard.

Navajo gila monster made of leopard stone by Roy Davis

Zuni horned lizard made of Ojo rock by Leroy Chavez

Zuni horned lizard made of stabilized turquoise by Brian Yatsattie

INSECTS

*Zuni dragonfly made of wood
by Alan Lewis*

Zuni caterpillar made of green snail shell

*Zuni spider made of elk antler
by Elton Kaamasee*

Despite their small size, insects are recognized in American Indian lore for their importance in fertilizing plants, their powerful stings, and the strength of their numbers. In Greek mythology, the young maiden Psyche was told to sort a mountain of seeds, a task which ants accomplished for her. When the hero of a Navajo story has been shattered into countless pieces, the ants collect all the tiny pieces so the hero can be restored. In the story of the Red Ant Way, ants brought the original herbs used to cure medical complaints.

Yet ants can cause great harm if molested. The Apache and some Pueblo peoples share similar beliefs about this. Accidentally eating an ant can bring on abdominal troubles, burning them can result in skin blisters, and spitting on an anthill can cause a sore throat. Violating other ant taboos might result in kidney, gallstone, or bladder problems.

Since ants, like spiders, were found everywhere, ants were often connected with travelling during premodern times. At Isleta, travelers were advised to feed ants before leaving the village; and at Zuni, turkey feather offerings were left in anthills while travelling. The Ant Society at Zuni is said to have certain curing powers, and the ant itself could help warriors by covering up their tracks. The Havasupai recommended that a woman who did not wish to become pregnant should urinate on a red ant hill. Among the Yaqui, an ant is one of the forms that the Creator can assume.

Among the Oglala Indians of the Plains, the butterfly (as well as the moth) was associated with the wind because both the insect and the wind are difficult to catch or contain. Cocoons came to represent the encapsulation of the whirlwind power of such insects. The Apache used butterfly motifs on their courting flutes. During the **Nawait** (nah-WAIT) ceremony held to bring life-giving summer rains, Tohono O'odham women painted their upper bodies with butterfly designs.

For many other tribes the butterfly was significant not only for the remarkable transformations it underwent from caterpillar to cocoon to butterfly, but for its associations with fertility. Before the Europeans introduced honeybees, the butterfly was

Zuni butterfly made of onyx by Michael Charley
(NOT TO SCALE)

Zuni scorpion made of Picasso marble by Todd Etsate

Then came forth a black tarantula magician.
In four places did he bite the earth, biting.
Some remaining shred of sickness he folded up and pounded into the earth and staked it down.

Then came forth the red wasp magicians.
In four places did they bite the earth, biting.
In four places they did make the earth into ollas and pounded them into the earth and staked it [sic] down.

Then came forth the little sleeping people [ants],
entering my house in endless journeys.
The illness food they did take and towards the north wind did they send it.

TOHONO O'ODHAM HEALING SONG
(From Underhill,
SINGING FOR POWER)

the primary pollinating insect in many areas of the Southwest. The Hopi honor it with the Butterfly Maiden (**Polik Mana**) dance. In Tohono O'odham legends, the creator **I'itoi** (EE-ee-toy) created butterflies to make the hearts of children happy. He made them out of flowers and fall leaves mixed with yellow pollen, white corn meal, green pine needles, sunlight, and bird songs—though the birds later made I'itoi give them back their songs.

Perhaps the most important insect in Indian mythologies is the spider. Warriors of the various Plains Indian tribes revered the spider's web for its ability to allow a bullet or an arrow to pass through, leaving the web virtually unharmed. Wisest of all creatures, the spider lives everywhere and travels everywhere—on, above, and below ground, as well as on water. To kill one is to risk being killed by lightning hurled by the thunder beings, although according to one ethnographer, the Maricopa Indians of the Gila River in Arizona once believed that killing a tarantula would help bring rain.

The Pueblo Keres Indians identify the creator as **Iatiko** (ee-AH-tee-ko), Thought Woman. She is usually represented in the form of Spider Grandmother in their creation story. Among the Hopi, however, Spider Woman (**Kokyang Wuhti**, KOK-yang WOH-tee) ruled all that was below and

Tawa (TAH-wah), Sun, ruled all that was above. Together, they willed all living things into being.

Spider Woman of the Navajo, taught women how to weave on a loom that her husband, Spider Man, made of sky and earth cords, sun rays, rock crystal, and sheet lightning. She also furnished the Twin War Gods with the formula for quieting the anger of one's enemies. When the waters of First World rose and began to flood, she wove a life-saving raft. Potentially dangerous but generally helpful, she gave the Twin War Gods feathers that represent the thread of life and saved them from danger.

In the Navajo creation story, insects were the people of First World. Six kinds of ants and three kinds of beetles lived in that dark underworld. In time, they were joined by the Locust People. When flood threatened the world, it was Locust who, with Badger and the Bighorn Sheep People, created a hole up into the next world. Spider Woman and Spider Ant held back the flood-waters. Other insects appeared later, such as the centipedes, who arose from the blood lost at the birth of the first big monsters (the **Yé'ii Tso**). A figure known in Navajo as **Begotsidi** (beh-go-TSEE-dee) is in charge of insects. In one story,

Zuni beetle made of abalone shell by Bernie Laselute

Zuni bee made of mother-of-pearl by Randy Lucio
(NOT TO SCALE)

*Zuni butterfly made of marble
by Jonathan Natewa*

Begotsidi was in charge of certain aspects of the creation and created, killed, and then restored to life the wasps. He can summon any insect at will and in several other Navajo stories disguises himself as one.

A bug called Black Body was allowed to use crystals to make the stars. His helpers, Little Beetle and Little White Beetle, cleaned and replaced each star daily, beginning in the East where they first begin to disappear at the end of night. A Hopi view of these black bugs teaches that if you behave really badly as a human, you will come back as a bug. According to both Zuni and Hopi tradition, a slow-moving type of black beetle is associated with storm clouds, as it is frequently seen on overcast days.

Big Fly (**Dontso**) is a type of fly that has a habit of alighting on one's shoulder, according to the Navajo. Appearing as a guardian figure in their curative sandpaintings, it is a powerful figure who often travels hidden behind the ear of the hero in legends, whispering valuable advice.

*Zuni grasshopper made of Picasso marble
by Michael Coble*

The locust does not appear often in Southwest Indian legends, but the Hopi used a locust medicine for treatment of wounds and to induce "true dreams." The locust also appears on some ritual items of the Flute Society. Both the locust and the cicada are candidates for the origin of Kokkopelli, the hump-backed flute player. They appear only after the rainy season has begun, the best time for travel and a time of fertility and growth for most plants. And the locust and the cicada both make music — of a sort.

Zuni scorpion made of fossilized ivory by Florentino Martinez

LIVESTOCK

My feet are made of mirage,
My bridle of strings of the sun.
My mane is like the white lightning.
My tail is like long black rain.
My eyes are big spreading stars.
My teeth are of the white shell.
My belly is white as dawnlight.
My heart is of everlasting garnet.

NAVAJO CHANT
(From Schevill, BEAUTIFUL ON
THE EARTH)

The introduction of domesticated livestock created a new category in the animal world of the Indians of the Southwest. Where once the world had been divided into prey animals and game animals, there were now domesticated animals who could be ridden, sheared, milked, or eaten. Just as game animals were ritually treated in a prescribed manner in order that their numbers would not diminish, so livestock animals had to be afforded some sort of ritual protection. The increase of herds became a vital concern.

Early livestock fetishes for protection and fertility included horses, cattle, sheep, and goats. In recent years this has expanded to include pigs and, for non-Indians, llamas, dogs, cats—even koi. Unlike the prey animal fetishes, where unworked stone pieces resembling or suggesting the animal may be most highly prized, accuracy is sometimes more important in livestock fetishes. Even a toy horse can be converted for use as a fetish and decorated with prayer feathers and stone and shell offerings.

Navajo mule made of Picasso marble by Jeffers Davies

Old Navajo livestock fetishes

During the winter solstice at Hopi, clay animals are buried in the corrals as prayers to increase the flocks and herds. Similar clay animal figurines, usually unfired, are used by many tribes in the Southwest during winter solstice ceremonies, often part of prayer rites to increase the herds of both domestic and wild animals. Also made are replicas of crops and money.

Carvings of livestock animals can have other purposes as well among the Navajo. A turquoise horse fetish is used in a series of ritual steps to ensure the birth of a very fast horse.

Navajo horse made of flourite by Everitt Pino

Navajo steer made of yellow mother-of-pearl by Roy Davis

Navajo ewe made of Picasso marble

PART III

OTHER FIGURES
AND OBJECTS

Zuni chile made of alabaster

CORN MAIDENS & CORN

First domesticated in the valley of Tehuacan in Mexico, corn spread northward and became a staple of the Indian diet in the Southwest by 1000 B.C. Unlike beans or squash, two other important food crops in the prehistoric era, corn will not re-seed itself but requires replanting each year. Perhaps in part because of the nurturing relationship required, corn has a position in Pueblo culture far above that of any other food source. Corn motifs are found on objects both utilitarian and ceremonial, in religious dances, clothing, mask designs, and on baskets and pottery.

Just as a mother nurtures her newborn with milk from her body, Corn Mother is honored for nurturing her people with the flesh of her body, corn. And her flesh is utilized in many ways. Corn pollen is used for blessings, prayers, offerings, marking ceremonial paths, as rain symbolism, and in payment for certain services. Corn husks are used for wrapping corn foods, for decorations on the masks of katsinas, and in making various types of prayerstick offerings. The colors of the six directions are the six colors of corns: yellow, white,

Oh my lovely mountain
My lovely mountain
High up in the sky
See the Rainmakers seated.
To here come the clouds now.
Behold around us
All will soon be a-bloom.
Where the flowers spring
Tall shall grow the youthful corn plants.

ZUNI CORN-GRINDING SONG
(From Curtis, SONGS AND LEGENDS OF THE AMERICAN INDIAN)

Zuni corn maiden made of stabilized turquoise by Faye Quandelacy
(NOT TO SCALE)

Pueblo maiden made of green snail shell by Faye Quandelacy

Reverse side of Pueblo maiden above, showing Corn Mother with corn maidens

red, blue, black, and speckled. It is ground, boiled, baked, dried, fried, parched, and popped.

Not surprisingly, the most widely held personal fetish among Pueblo peoples in the Southwest is a perfect ear of corn. Called a **mille** (MEE-leh) by the Zuni (**miwi** is the plural form), a perfect ear of corn is one in which the kernels cover the entire ear of corn, including the very tip. When surrounded by feathers, it symbolizes life and the life-giving force of the Creator. White or blue corn is most frequently used, but regardless of the color, they are usually wrapped in cotton or buckskin and carefully stored when not in use.

The **ciwika** (SEE-wee-ka) fetish of the Tewa medicine man is a perfect ear of white corn. At Hopi naming ceremonies, a perfect ear of white corn is used and then presented to the infant and kept for life. The Zuni **tiponi** has a perfect ear of blue corn as its base. At Cochiti a perfect ear of corn was an ear of blue corn with the tassels still attached. Called a yaya (see "The Rio Grande Pueblos," p. 13), it is kept by the owner for life. After the owner's death, the kernels are removed and mixed in with kernels to be used for planting in the coming year in the belief that the power will be absorbed by the corn and bring a better crop. There is a similar practice at Zuni.

At Isleta the Corn Mothers are wrapped with cotton, dressed with stone and shell beads, and given prayer feathers during winter purification ceremonies. Among the seven Keresan pueblos, which include Santo Domingo and Zia, Thought Woman said corn was her heart and gave it to the people. The most important fetish among these people is Iarrikko, the perfect ear of corn, said to represent Iatiko herself. Among the Tiwas, the Corn Mother is known as **Iamaparuh** (ee-AH-ma-pa-ru) and her fetish is **keideh** (KEE-deh).

Corn is cared for by the women at most pueblos. Some women even sing gently to the corn. At some pueblos, a long perfect ear of yellow corn represents the male, and a shorter double-ear of white corn represents the female. They are placed together in the corn storerooms to ensure an abundant supply of corn for the winter and on into the following summer until the next harvest.

Stone fetishes resembling an ear of corn and symbolizing the power of the Corn Mother were once widely held among the pueblos. In some instances, the eyes and mouths were carved and inlaid with turquoise or shell. Sometimes the tapered, cylindrical stone would simply be dressed in shell and stone beads and wrapped with the appropriate feathers. It is most probable

Zuni corn maiden made of stabilized turquoise by Sandra Quam
(NOT TO SCALE)

Zuni corn maidens made of fossilized ivory by Sandra Quandelacy

Blue evening falls
Blue evening falls
Nearby, in every direction
It sets the corn tassels trembling.

TOHONO O'ODHAM SONG
(From Underhill, SINGING
FOR POWER)

Zuni corn maiden made of mother-of-pearl
by Eugene Bowekaty

that the stone objects found in ancient Pueblo sites and once labeled as phallic objects are really Corn Mothers.

Zuni legend says corn was brought by **Paiyatemu** (pai-YAH-teh-moo), an assistant to the Sun. There were eight Corn Maiden sisters, though some say there were originally six, being joined later by sweet corn and squash for the total of eight. Still others say there were seven, related to the seven Star Maidens, symbolized by the Pleiades. In any case, the Corn Maidens left Zuni because they were not being given prayer offerings or properly respected. It was Paiyatemu who eventually found them and brought them back. At Zuni there is a ceremony in winter called the **Molaaweh** (spelled mola:we in Zuni linguistic transcription, pronounced moe-LAH-h'-weh) held during the winter solstice in which young women take the role of the Corn Maidens to symbolize the ritual return of corn.

At Hopi the sun is addressed as Sun Father and corn as Corn Mother, with the ears of corn being her children. Though there are references to Corn People, corn itself is regarded as female. In certain religious contexts, an individual who has come of age or has been initiated is said to have "become corn," indicating that they have matured and become a fully realized person. A perfect ear of corn here, as at most pueblos, is an important personal fetish, given during the naming ceremony and kept for life.

According to the Hopi, corn was brought by Masau'u, the deity associated with the underworld and death (see "Rabbits"). Among many pueblos there is a striking connection between corn, death, and renewal. A few brief examples: at Cochiti corn was once placed next to the body of one who had just died to represent their heart, and at Jemez an ear of corn was hung on a nearby wall when a woman went into labor. At Zuni there is a large body of ritual poetry which speaks of Corn giving her flesh to nurture her Zuni children and instructing them to bury the "flesh" of the corn as they bury the flesh of their human dead. In this way, new corn will spring forth from the flesh of the "dead" corn, the **tah-ah** (TAH-ah) "seed of seeds."

In one version of the Navajo creation story, a deity who was transformed from an ear of corn created the universe. In the Navajo Beauty Way ceremonial (said to be named for the beautiful white sand in which one of the maidens left her footprints) there is a story that the younger of the two fleeing sisters stopped in many places during her journey and was offered food at each stop. But

Zuni corn maiden made of jet by Sandra Quandelacy
(NOT TO SCALE)

Zuni mother and child made of fossilized ivory by Sandra Quandelacy

the only people with whom she ate were the Corn People, who fed her with corn, squash, beans, and melons. The Navajo also use corn meal and corn pollen in their religious observances, and corn (**nah-tah**) is one of the four sacred plants. According to an old Navajo custom, the twin ear of corn recognized by the Zuni as a female corn is not to be eaten by a pregnant woman lest she bear twins.

CRYSTALS

Diagnosticians and healers among many tribes in the Southwest use crystals for shedding light in a figurative sense. Such uses include determining the cause of illness, locating missing objects, locating the trail of an enemy, finding the place in the body where an illness lies, and ceremonially lighting prayer sticks. At Isleta, crystals were believed to symbolize or invoke the power of the moon. Both crystals and white quartz pebbles belonging to the Tewa winter chiefs represented ice and were referred to as "ice mothers." The crystals that are occasionally seen today attached to fetishes have been added in response to the New Age market and are not an Indian tradition.

Quartz crystal

Rock crystal

Navajo bobcat made of pipestone, with arrowhead, by Roy Davis

ARROWHEADS

Often associated with lightning and believed to be the point with which it strikes, found arrowheads and larger lance points or stone knives are highly prized. A made point does not have the association with lightning that a found point does.

Among the Rio Grande Pueblos, a medicine person may hold a stone point in one hand to protect himself while going through the appointed ritual for a patient or the tribe. At Isleta, the medicine man once carried a stone point when outdoors to guard against evil during night ceremonies. Among the Havasupai, an arrowhead or sharp flake of obsidian was attached to a cap or a shirt to ward off illness.

At Isleta Pueblo, among other pueblos, a runner once carried a white arrowpoint in his mouth for speed and protection. Arrowpoints are sometimes suspended from a cradleboard to protect an infant, particularly among the Navajo and at Acoma. Additionally, an arrowpoint (preferably white) can be worn around the neck under a shirt, in one's hair, or attached to a woman's belt for protection against witches and related evil. Yuman tribes, such as the Maricopa, traditionally warned against carrying a found arrowpoint because it could attract lightning.

Arrowpoints added to a fetish sometimes indicate that it is one of the Zuni prey gods. It can also be added, according to the traditions of other pueblos, as a protection for the fetish itself or as part of an attached bundle that strengthens the fetish. One of the many types of Zuni corn fetishes has a stone point attached to it to prevent sickness that a witch might inflict.

CONCRETIONS

For hunting or prey fetishes, a stone which naturally resembled an animal was generally much more highly prized than a carved one. Even today some fetish carvers will occasionally look for a stone that already has some resemblance to the animal they wish to carve. In addition to the value of these unusual stone formations due to their resemblance to animals, concretions are also highly prized for their resemblance to important body organs or simply for their uniqueness. They are likely to be owned by the Pueblo or a religious society and to be entrusted to the care of a cacique.

HUMAN & OTHER FIGURINES

Carvers sometimes create human-like figures carved of stone or antler. While most are simply representations of people, there is reason to believe that some may be derived from similar figures used on altars set up by various religious societies at Zuni for certain ceremonies. These figures usually have an arrowhead attached, either to symbolize the protective presence afforded by the figurine or to represent a cacique who carries an arrowpoint for protection during a ceremony.

A pair of male and female fetish figurines were once used at Zuni in ceremonies for a woman who needed protection against losing her unborn children to miscarriage or stillborn deliveries. A woman who had trouble conceiving could request a ceremony that used a figure with a bead attached to the waist (symbolizing pregnancy) in the rite.

Navajo singers wrap both light- and dark-banded cylindrical aragonite stones in multi-colored yarn and use them in connection with certain healing ceremonies. The light stone represents the female and the dark the male. The Navajo also make

Zuni human figurine by Hayes Leekya
(NOT TO SCALE)

Zuni human figurine made of natural turquoise by Sarah Leekya

animals of clay, wood, mud, or ground corn to ward off the consequences of a relatively minor violation of an animal-related taboo.

The Yuman people believed that dreaming of certain plants could cause illness. One called **i'iusha** (ee-YU-sha) could cause chills and fever. The shaman would carve an image of the patient out of ironwood to use in the curing rite.

MISCELLANY

An enemy's equipment could be used as a fetish object in either protection or war-related rituals. At one time, some among the Hopi used captured Navajo weapons in this manner. In a similar vein, enemy scalps were regarded as sources of power and occasionally treated as fetishes or talismans. Groups from the Tohono O'odham to the Zuni kept the scalps in special jars under specialized ownership for use in specific ceremonies. At Isleta, they were used to cure toothaches. Other groups used them in connection with war ceremonials—for purifying someone who had killed an enemy or against witchcraft.

Shells are usually attached to fetishes as part of an offering or used to hold water and sacred corn meal or pollen in rites. In rare instances, they can be fetishes themselves. A large conch shell is used at Zuni as a fetish connected with rain.

Feathers are used in some aspects of most Southwest Indian religious rites. They may be used in purification, as part of a prayer offering, attached to a fetish as a sacred plume (called **lah-sho-an-nih** in Zuni), or worn. They are not,

Zuni hand pendant made of turquoise by Carmelia Snow

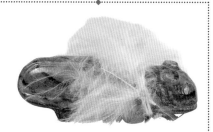

Zuni serpentine puma with feathers, made by Lorandina Sheche

however, a fetish or amulet. For further discussion, see "Birds."

Fetishes are often carried in buckskin pouches or stored in pottery jars, but the container itself is not a fetish nor is it a religious object by itself. The fetish jars on the market are made strictly for sale. There is good reason to believe that even many of those acquired in the 1800s and appearing to be of great antiquity were, in fact, made to satisfy the demands of a persistent trader, collector, or ethnologist.

PART IV

MATERIALS

Zuni bison made of azurite malachite
by Lynn Quam

MATERIALS

Some of the materials used by Southwest Indian groups in the past were found within the traditional boundaries of the tribes that utilized them, but many more were traded in from distant areas. Seashells from the Sea of Cortez and the Pacific Coast were traded throughout the Greater Southwest over well-established trading routes in prehistoric times. Turquoise also found its way into the hands of artisans who lived at great distances from the places where it was mined.

The range of materials used prior to the arrival of the Spanish in the sixteenth century and of those used as recently as the early 1970s was largely the same. Coral is the notable exception. There was no red coral available to Southwest Indian artisans before the Spanish introduced Mediterranean coral. Due to over-harvesting and pollution in the Mediterranean Sea, coral is now imported from the waters of the Sea of Japan.

Lorandina Sheche grinding a fetish

In addition to the more readily available materials such as antler, clay, and occasionally bone, an array of seashells was used—most notably red abalone, conus, spondylus (better known as spiny oyster shell), and glycemeris shell. The size and thickness of the shells limited the size of the carvings. Artisans favored sea shells over freshwater shells for jewelry and religious purposes, most probably because of the association with the seemingly limitless waters of the ocean, reverentially esteemed and recognized by these desert dwellers

Lorandina Sheche polishing a fetish

as the source of the summer rains. Among the more commonly used new additions to the shell supply are green snail, a color range of mother-of-pearl, and cowry shell.

It is not surprising that the trade routes bringing all kinds of shells and stones to Indian craftspeople now extend worldwide. Zooisite from South America, charoite from Siberia, sugilite from the Kalahari Desert, lapis lazuli from Afghanistan, malachite from Africa, and magnetite from Europe, as well as pieces of meteorite from outer space—all have found their way to the workbenches of Southwest Indians.

Although artisans who now carve for the buying public employ all types of materials and techniques, traditional carvers selected stones and other materials less for ease of working than for their color and associated properties. Some of the less frequently used traditional materials were as ephemeral as corn meal or as substantial as unusually shaped concretions the size of small boulders. Some of the most ancient and sacred fetishes include fossils and fossil casts, many associated with specific deities or mountains. The section below lists features and related facts about the more frequently worked stones and minerals used by Indian artists of both yesterday and today.

TRADITIONAL STONES & OTHER MATERIALS

Agate: SiO_2 A form of fibrous cryptocrystalline quartz, this silica mineral is a type of chalcedony, like flint and **chert**, which is a granular form. Naturally colored in warm tones by iron oxides, like onyx, agate can also be dyed. Chert and flint are dull, while chalcedony is lustrous, the only difference between them. Chert is said to be usually lighter than flint but is otherwise similar in most properties except for brittleness and the fractures of chert being more splintery. Chert is sometimes called hornstone, a term used for any impure flinty rock, including jasper. Jasper is the same, only colored by hematite inclusions. Carnelian is a red chalcedony.

Ancient European tradition claimed that an agate made the wearer bold, persuasive, and prudent, bringing God's favor and the power to overcome enemies and gain wealth. White agate was thought to be a cure for insomnia. Ancient Greek mariners wore chalcedony amulets as a talisman against drowning. Brazil and Uruguay are the largest current sources for agate. See **Onyx**.

Alabaster: $CaSO_4.2H_2O$ A hydrous calcium sulfate, this is a fine-grained, massive form of gypsum, commonly running to warmer colors and occasionally with pale green. Most types used in carving are from New Mexico, Colorado, and Utah. It's often confused with marble, which is a hydrous calcium carbonate limestone. See **Marble**.

Sheep made of alabaster by Marlo Booqua

Amber: $C_{10}H_{16}O$ This oxygenated hydrocarbon is a fossilized tree resin, ranging from clear to opaque in brownish yellow to yellowish white. It is sometimes imitated using a mixture of tree sap and petrochemical resins. Most amber comes from the Baltic area.

Anhydrite: $CaSO_4$ An anhydrous calcium sulfate harder than many other gypsum minerals, anhydrite ranges from almost white to a powder blue often sold as angelite.

Aragonite: $CaCo_3$ This form of calcium carbonate named for a deposit in Spain is also found in Colorado, Arizona, and New Mexico. It changes structure under normal temperatures and eventually becomes calcite, which is stable. The pearly layer of many shells is composed of aragonite, the outside calcite.

Azurite: $Cu_3(Co_3)_2(OH)_2$ A copper carbonate that appears in various shades of blue, mostly deep blue, azurite is sometimes mistaken for lapis lazuli. Found with malachite, a more common copper mineral than azurite, in New Mexico and Arizona.

Basalt: This igneous rock is composed of microscopic grains of soda-lime feldspar with pyroxene (an iron ore) with other minerals often intruding.

Calcite: $CaCo_3$ A crystalline form of calcium carbonate, calcite includes spar, rhodochrosite, limestone, marble, and chalk.

Chalcosiderite: $CuO.3Fe_2O_3.2P_2O_5.9H_2O$ Sometimes called white turquoise, chalcosiderite is actually not turquoise but is very closely related, containing iron rather than the aluminum in turquoise. The material used by Southwest Indian artists comes mostly from southeast Arizona.

Charoite: A calcium potassium silicate found with inclusions of tinaksite (orange), augite (black), and feldspar (white) that was discovered near the Chara River in eastern Siberia in 1976.

Chrysocolla: $CuSiO_3.2H_2O$ Sometimes confused with turquoise, this blue-green hydrous copper silicate may be banded and often appears to be somewhat translucent because of its crystalline nature. It's usually found with copper, malachite, and azurite and is mined in Arizona, with striking examples found at the Bisbee Mine.

Chrysoprase: A form of quartz, this apple-green chalcedony gets its color from nickel oxide. In the Middle Ages of Europe, it was believed that a thief about to be beheaded or hanged could escape his executioner if he placed the stone in his mouth. See **Agate**.

Zuni bear made of dolomite by Marilyn Chuyate

Clay: This term is used to refer to any substance made of micro-scopic particles (1/256 of an inch or less in diameter) that becomes plastic when wet. A major ingredient of clay and claystones is kaolinite (better known as kaolin), a hydrous aluminum silicate that is pure white in its pure form.

Dolomite: $CaMg(CO_3)_2$ Usually banded and warm in color, dolomite may sometimes include black and green. The form most often used in carvings is opaque, although it can also be transparent. If it contains manganese and iron, it's called ankerite. Found in Missouri and New York, as well as Mexico. See **Limestone**.

Fluorite: CaF_2 A calcium fluoride, this crystalline material is also called fluorspar. It is relatively translucent and ranges from nearly colorless to blue and green, occasionally with warmer shades and banding. Found in many areas of the Midwest and West.

Gaspeite: $(NiMgFe)CO_3$ The type used most frequently by Southwest Indian artisans is a nickel carbonate colored by iron and magnesium that is almost chartreuse in color. Named for the Gaspé Peninsula in Canada where it was first identified, most comes from the Kambalda nickel mine in western Australia.

Glass: Made from pure silica that can be colored by the presence of various minerals, including metallic oxides.

Gold slag: A red transparent-to-opaque glass by-product of gold refining.

Gypsum: $CaSO_4.2H_2O$ This is a hydrous calcium sulfate that occurs in forms from alabaster (which is opaque) to selenite (which appears as a color-less translucent crystal). Gypsum is commonly found in many locales.

Hematite: Fe_2O_3 An iron oxide that may appear in a form called clay iron-stone used for carving. The crystalline form called specular hematite was a valuable trading commodity between many of the Pueblo tribes up to the early 1900s because of its uses as a paint for certain religious objects and as an offering.

The name comes from the Greek word meaning blood. Called bloodstone in early Europe because of its color, it was believed to help staunch the flow of blood from wounds.

Indian paintstone: See **Clay**.

Jet: A form of the bituminous mineral coal called lignite. Lignite is brown, however, and mineralogy texts list jet as "a black variety of brown coal."

Zuni skunk made of jet by David Tsikeewa

Lapis lazuli: $(Na, Ca)_4(AlSiO_4)_3$-(So_4, S, Cl) This popular stone contains lazurite as well as varying proportions of calcite, pyroxene, and iron pyrite (the iron sulfide crystal commonly known as fool's gold). The Blue Wrinkle Mine near Crested Butte, Colorado, produces a very pale grade of lapis. The only other known source in the western hemisphere for this variety is in Chile. Most lapis lazuli comes from Afghanistan and other South Asian sites, and there are prolific deposits around Lake Baikal in Siberia. Lighter grades have recently been dubbed "denim lapis." Once used in Europe as a cure for melancholy. See **Sodalite**.

Lepidolite: $K_2Li_3Al_3(AlSi_3O_{10})_2$-$(OH, F)_4$ Surprisingly part of the mica group of minerals, lepidolite ranges from pale shades of pink to yellow to purple. Most of the lepidolite in current use comes from a quarry on the Pala Indian Reservation in California. It is mined as a source of lithium.

Limestone: A sedimentary rock composed of calcite, which may also have magnesium carbonate. Marble is a metamorphic and more compact form of limestone.

Magnesite: $MgCO_3$ Also called magnesium carbonate, magnesite is a form of hard limestone. The pure white color is preferred by carvers and jewelers (who use it for inlay material), but it can range into warm brown shades if colored by iron oxides. Much of what is in current use is mined in California.

Malachite: $Cu_2Co_3(OH)_2$ A form of copper carbonate that ranges from light to deep green and is usually banded. It can be found with azurite, a rarer form of copper carbonate. Although found in Arizona, Utah, and Nevada, much is now imported from Zaire.

*Zuni puma made of malachite
by Leland Boone*

Charms carved of malachite were used in Europe and the Middle East to ward off the evil eye. Regarded as an appropriate talisman for children, it was also believed to protect its wearer from falling, like turquoise. If carved with the image of the sun, it would protect the wearer from venomous snakes and evil spells.

Marble: Pure marble, a carbonate, is white, but impurities in the rock can produce a range of colors. The term "marble" includes all crystalline calcium carbonate and calcium magnesium carbonate rocks that can take a high polish. It is basically a massive crystalline aggregate composed of hardened or metamorphosed limestone. The color depends upon the minerals occurring with it.

Onyx: See **Travertine** and **Agate**. Used as an amulet in the Middle Ages to ward off the evil eye.

Opal: $SiO_2.nH_2O$ A silicon dioxide, similar to quartz, opal can include iron or aluminum, which affects the color and its intensity. (In its pure form opal is white.) Common opal, which is partially translucent and generally milky, occurs in many regions and is the form used more often than precious opal from Australia, boulder opal from British Columbia, or fire opal from Mexico.

Paintstone: See **Clay**.

Petrified wood: Wood whose organic material has been replaced with silica oxide and colored by the presence of various minerals over millions of years. The best known deposit is in Petrified Forest National Park in Arizona. At Jemez, old fragments and pieces are dressed in feathers and stone and shell beads for ritual use. Use at other pueblos range from associations with the goddess of game to war rituals. See **Agate**.

Picasso marble: A type of marble that has distinctive, often angular brown, black, and white markings. Found in Utah. See **Marble**.

Navajo horse made of pipestone

Pipestone: A red-brown-to-white clay-like mineral also known as catlinite. The primary source is in Pipestone, Minnesota, now a national monument. The name refers to its use as a material from which pipes were carved. It was so important and so widely traded that even traditional enemies laid down their weapons when entering the quarry area.

Prystine: See **Magnesite**.

Rhodochrosite: $MnCO_3$ A mottled pink manganese carbonate related to calcite, this stone is generally banded and can have delicate, almost lacy markings. Found in conjunction with silver, manganese, copper, and lead, much of the stone came from mines in Colorado, Montana, Nevada; but most of that used by carvers today comes from Argentina.

Rhyolite: An igneous rock with quartz and alkali feldspar, occasionally with magnetite, rhyolite ranges in color from grey to pinkish to brown. Can be banded and therefore is often confused with fine-grain sandstone. See **Sandstone**.

Riccolite: A banded form of serpentine found in southern New Mexico. See **Serpentine**.

Sandstone: A sedimentary mix of quartz with silica, carbonates, or iron oxides, the latter affecting the intensity of its brownish hues. They're used occasionally for fetishes, usually painted after carving to add the necessary features.

Selenite: $CaSO_4.2H_2O$ A hydrous calcium sulfate that is simply another form of gypsum. See **Gypsum**.

Septarian: A yellowish-to-white calcite cluster usually found in a grey to brown limestone matrix. Utah is its primary source.

Serpentine: $Mg_6(Si_4O_{10})(OH)_8$ This hydrous magnesium silicate ranges from yellow green to deep green, to brown, black, and grey. It can be speckled, banded (called riccolite), mottled, or evenly colored, as well as colored by the presence of iron and magnesium. Carvers often use serpentine from New Mexico.

Navajo otter made of serpentine by Roy Davis

Soapstone: $Mg_3(Si_4O_{10})(OH)_2$ Also known as steatite, soapstone is a hydrous magnesium silicate — a form of talc — that is used only infrequently by carvers. It tends to run from almost white to dark green. Serpentine is often misidentified as soapstone.

Sodalite: $Na_4(AlSiO_4)_3Cl$ A sodium aluminum silicate with chlorine that runs from blue-grey to blue and is occasionally mistaken for lapis lazuli. See **Lapis lazuli**.

Sugilite: $(K, Na)(Na, Fe+3)_2(Li_2Fe+3)Si_{12}O_{30}$ This recent addition to the carvers' inventories is composed of alkali metals, iron, aluminum, water, and manganese. Yellow brown (found in Japan) to purple (found in the Kalahari Desert of southern Africa). Also known as royal azel and royal lavulite. Similar to sogdianite, but sogdianite has zirconium and sugilite does not.

Tagua nut: Also known as "vegetable ivory," because it's the fruit of the ivory or tagua palm that grows in the tropical northern regions of South

America, from Panama to Peru. When young, the nut is soft and edible. As it "cures," it becomes extremely hard, and its working properties and markings closely resemble those of ivory. In the late 1800s these "ivory nuts" were made into everything their size would permit, from thimbles to needle cases and especially buttons.

Travertine: $CaCo_3$ A crystalline carbonate, banded form of limestone, usually a mix of calcite and/or aragonite, travertine is usually creamy white to beige in color. It's found in deposits around calcareous springs and is sometimes called Mexican onyx or onyx marble.

Turquoise: $CuAl_6(PO_4)_4\text{-}(OH)_8.4H_2O$ This popular hydrous aluminum phosphate, colored by copper salts, ranges from pale green to deep blue, even in the same stone. Turquoise is found in all shades of green and blue, which lend

themselves to associations with sky and water, as well as with the direction west. Primary sources for turquoise nowadays include China, Iran, and the southwestern United States (New Mexico, Colorado, Arizona, and Nevada). It is sometimes confused with the more glassy chrysocolla, which has a more crystalline structure.

Zuni dinosaur made of shell, turquoise and alabaster by Leonard Halate

The Navajo identify blue turquoise as male and green turquoise as female, but this is not a restriction on which sex can wear which color. Color is a matter of personal preference, though collective preference seems to place a higher value on the stronger blue shades, depending on the markings or matrix of the stone. This, too, is a matter of personal preference, and some people prefer no matrix whatsoever.

Chemicals or coloring agents can change the color and/or harden turquoise so it can be worked more easily. Treated stone is more likely to be found in fetish carvings or bead and pendant necklaces than found set in silver. Stone which has been treated may be called "treated turquoise" or by one of the more recently coined terms designed to remove the stigma of treatment, such as "stabilized," "fracture-sealed," or "enhanced." Most turquoise is mined by

Zuni bear made of stabilized turquoise by Lena Boone

blasting these days and therefore contains fracture lines. If the stone is badly fractured or is too soft for practical use, it will be immersed, usually in a plastic resin, to harden it. There is nothing wrong with treated turquoise providing it is identified as such and priced accordingly. It is easier for the craftsperson to use and, in the case of carving, more resistant to wear and tear. While a good piece of treated turquoise can be worth more than a poor grade of natural turquoise, the best treated turquoise will never come remotely close to the quality and value of the best natural turquoise.

According to ancient European traditions, turquoise could prevent its wearer from falling, although that was later amended to apply only to turquoise set in gold. In both the Middle East and thirteenth-century Europe, it was used to protect horses. By the seventeenth century in Europe, it was worn almost exclusively by men. As with diamonds, people believed that turquoise would retain its special powers only if gifted. If it was sold, the spirit fled the stone.

Variscite: $Al(Po_4).2H_2O$ A hydrous aluminum phosphate that is sometimes mistaken for turquoise but is greener and contains no copper. Very pale shades have been marketed as "white turquoise," as happened with chalcosiderite. It was first discovered in Germany; in the U. S. it can be found primarily in Utah and Nevada.

Wood: Everything from snake to mountain lion fetishes can be made of wood. Cedar, juniper, pine, and cottonwood are among the range of trees used. In many instances, the preferred wood is from a tree struck by lightning.

SHELLS

Abalone: The more common and readily available red abalone is most frequently used, although abalone also appears in green. Not only is it used for fetishes and jewelry, but the whole shell, if in tact, can be used in religious rituals.

Coral: $CaCo_3(Mg)$ A calcium carbonate (calcite) with magnesium, created by colonies of the marine coral polyp. Originally most red coral was imported from the Mediterranean but pollution and over-harvesting has eliminated that source. Today most coral for carving and jewelry comes from the Sea of Japan. Heat or ammonia can turn it irreversibly white. The larger the piece, the smoother and more even the surface, and the deeper the color, the more expensive the coral. In recent years, delicate pink "angel-skin" coral and creamy pale orange shades have become more sought after and therefore more expensive.

Like most red stones, coral was believed to help staunch bleeding. Ancient European custom also held that it afforded safety in crossing rivers, cured madness, and bestowed wisdom.

Cowry shell: There are many varieties of this small gastro-pod (snail). One variety, *Cypraea moneta*, was used for centuries as a form of currency in Asia and Africa.

Zuni armadillo made of cowry shell and serpentine by Fabian Homer

Glycymeris: A large bivalve (clam) used since prehistoric times and traded into the Southwest from the coasts of present-day

California and Baja California. The Hohokam carved them into pendants and frog forms. The top was ground away to make bangle bracelets. Laevicardium is another large, thick bivalve also used for carving and jewelry by prehistoric peoples in the Southwest.

Mother-of-pearl: This substance occurs in both bivalves and mollusks and comes in a range of colors — white, yellow, purple, and black. The shiny, nacreous inner layer of the shells is composed chiefly of aragonite, while the outer shell is calcite. Exposure to harsh chemicals and soaps will convert the aragonite to calcite, causing the shell to loose its luster.

Zuni fish made of mother-of-pearl by Terry Banteah

Spondylus: Commonly known as spiny oyster shell, spondylus comes from the Pacific coast of Baja California and the northwestern coast of South America. Until the Spanish introduced coral, it was highly prized for its orange to reddish-orange to red colors because it was the only source for these shades. *Spondylus pictorum* is the red variety. *Spondylus calcifer* is known as "purple lip" for the band of deep purple along the outer rim.

REFERENCES

Bunzel, Ruth L.

1992   *Zuni Ceremonialism*. Originally published in 1932 in the *47th Annual Bureau of American Ethnology Report*, 1929-1930. Albuquerque: University of New Mexico Press.

Curtis, Natalie, collector and trans.

1968   *Songs and Legends of the American Indian*. Original edition, 1907. New York: Dover Publications.

Cushing, Frank Hamilton

1994   *Zuni Fetishes*. Original edition, 1883. Las Vegas: KC Publications.

Densmore, Frances

1942   *Teton Sioux Music*. Bureau of American Ethnology Bulletin, No. 61.

Goddard, Pliny Earle

1933   *Navajo Texts*. Anthropological Papers of the American Museum of Natural History, Vol. 34.

Haile, Berard

1947   *Navajo Sacrificial Figurines*. Chicago: University of Chicago Press.

Kunz, George Frederick

1942   *The Curious Lore of Precious Stones*. Original edition, 1913. New York: Dover Publications.

Laski, Vera

1959   "Seeking Life" in *Memoirs of the American Folklore Society*, Vol. 50.
        Philadelphia: American Folklore Society.

Rasmussen, Knud

1931   "The Netsalik Eskimo," *Report of the Fifth Thule Expedition*.
        Copenhagen.

Spinden, Herbert Joseph, trans.

1976   *Songs of the Tewas*. Original edition, 1933. Santa Fe, NM:
        Sunstone Press.

Stirling, Matthew N.

1942   *Origin Myths of Acoma and Other Records*. Bureau of American
        Ethnology, Bulletin No. 135. Washington, D.C.: Smithsonian
        Institution.

Tedlock, Dennis, trans.

1978   *Finding the Center: Narrative Poetry of the Zuni Indians*. Omaha:
        University of Nebraska Press.

Underhill, Ruth M.

        *Singing for Power: The Song Magic of the Papago Indians of Southern
        Arizona*. Original copyright, 1930. Tucson: University of Arizona
        Press.

CHART A: MEDIEVAL LORE ASSOCIATED WITH DAYS OF THE WEEK

	SUNDAY	MONDAY	TUESDAY	WEDNESDAY	THURSDAY	FRIDAY	SATURDAY
COLOR	yellow	white	red	green	violet	blue	black
ANIMAL	lion	ermine	lynx	fox	bull	goat	hog
PLANET	Sun	Moon	Mars	Mercury	Jupiter	Venus	Saturn
AGE	adolescence	infancy	adulthood	youth	old age	childhood	decrepitude
STONE	chrysolite	pearl	ruby	emerald	sapphire	sapphire	diamond

YELLOW
For men: secrecy, appropriate for a silent lover
For women: generosity

WHITE*
For men: friendship, religion, integrity
For women: contemplation, affability, purity

RED
For men: command, nobility, lordship, vengeance
For women: pride, obstinancy, haughtiness

GREEN**
For men: joyousness, transitory hope, decline of friendship
For women: unfounded ambition, childish delight, change

VIOLET
For men: sober judgement, industry, gravity
For women: high thoughts, piety

BLUE
For men: wisdom, high & magnanimous thoughts
For women: jealosy in love, politeness, vigilance

BLACK
For men: gravity, good sense, constancy, fortitude
For married women: constant love, perseverance
For young women: fickleness, foolishness

* Among Greeks and Romans, the color of mourning. Italian widows once wore a white band around the head.
** Associated with transitory verdant spring.

TRIBE	EAST	SOUTH	WEST	NORTH	ZENITH	NADIR
NAVAJO	White Male Rain Dark Clouds Black Thunder Doves Elk, Skunk, Bear, Porcupine Blanca Peak White Shell	Blue/Green Dark Mist Female Rain Bluebirds Deer, Beaver, Puma, Chipmunk Mt.Taylor Turquoise	Red/Yellow Dark Clouds Male Rain Yellow Warbler San Francisco Peak Abalone Shell	Black Dark Mist Female Rain Blackbird Hesperus Peak Jet		
SANTA ANA	White Wolf	Red Bobcat	Blue Bear	Yellow/Brown Puma	All Colors Eagle	Black Shrew
ZIA	Buffalo	Mountain Sheep	Antelope	Deer		
ZUNI -HUNTING -INITIATION -PROTECTION	White Wolf Wolf Wolf House of the Day Dawn Land	Red Wildcat/Jaguar Wildcat Badger House of Red Sunrise Summer Land	Blue Bear Yellow Coyote Bear Blue Home of the Waters Night Land	Yellow Puma Puma Puma Home of the Barren Regions Winter Land	All Colors Eagle Eagle Eagle Sky Land of Light	Black Shrew Shrew Shrew Under World Land of Darkness
APACHE	Black	Blue/Green	Red/Yellow	White		
TAOS	Wolf White	Wildcat Blue	Bear Yellow	Puma Blue		
TEWA	White Wolf	Red Badger	Yellow Bear	Blue Puma	All Colors Eagle	Black Shrew/Gopher
HOPI	White White Wolf Magpie	Red Yellow/Red Wildcat Parrot	Blue Blue Bear Blubird	Yellow Black Puma Oriole	Black Eagle Tanager	All Colors Shrew

TITLES OF RELATED INTEREST FROM TREASURE CHEST BOOKS

ALSO BY MARK BAHTI –

Navajo Sandpainting Art. 1999. Completely revised edition of Bahti's fascinating look at Navajo ceremonial art. Fully illustrated, paperback. ISBN 1-887896-05-8

Pueblo Stories and Storytellers. Bahti's enormously popular book about story-teller figurines with a delightful selection of Pueblo Indian legends. Fully illustrated, paperback. ISBN 1-887896-01-5

Southwest Indian Designs. Bahti presents more than 200 Southwest Indian designs and the peoples who created them. Fully illustrated, paperback. ISBN 0-918080-51-7

OTHER OUTSTANDING BOOKS –

A Guide to Navajo Weavings by Kent McManis and Robert Jeffries. Heavily illustrated, paperback. ISBN 1-887896-07-4

A Guide to Zuni Fetishes & Carvings, Vol. I: The Animals and the Carvers and *Vol II: The Materials and the Carvers* by Kent McManis. Heavily illustrated, paperback. ISBN 1-887896-14-7/ISBN 1-887896-11-2

Lakota: An Illustrated History by Sergio Macedo. The story of the Lakota Sioux of the Great Plains in graphic-novel form. Paperback. ISBN 1-887896-02-3

The Legacy of a Master Potter: Nampeyo and Her Descendants by Mary Ellen and Laurence Blair. A long-awaited study of the Hopi-Tewa potter who revived the fine art of Hopi pottery making. Heavily illustrated, paperback. ISBN 1-887896-06-6

San Xavier Del Bac: An Artist's Portfolio by Sharon Wright Pettus. An intimate look at the unique "colonial baroque" folkart of this world-famous Spanish mission, with introduction. Hardcover. ISBN 1-887896-04-X

Taos Pueblo: A Walk Through Time by John J. Bodine. A gem of a tourbook of the village itself along with a concise history of the Taos Indians. Vintage duotone photographs. Paperback. ISBN 1-887896-00-7